Cats Butts

COLORING BOOK

This Book

BELONGS TO

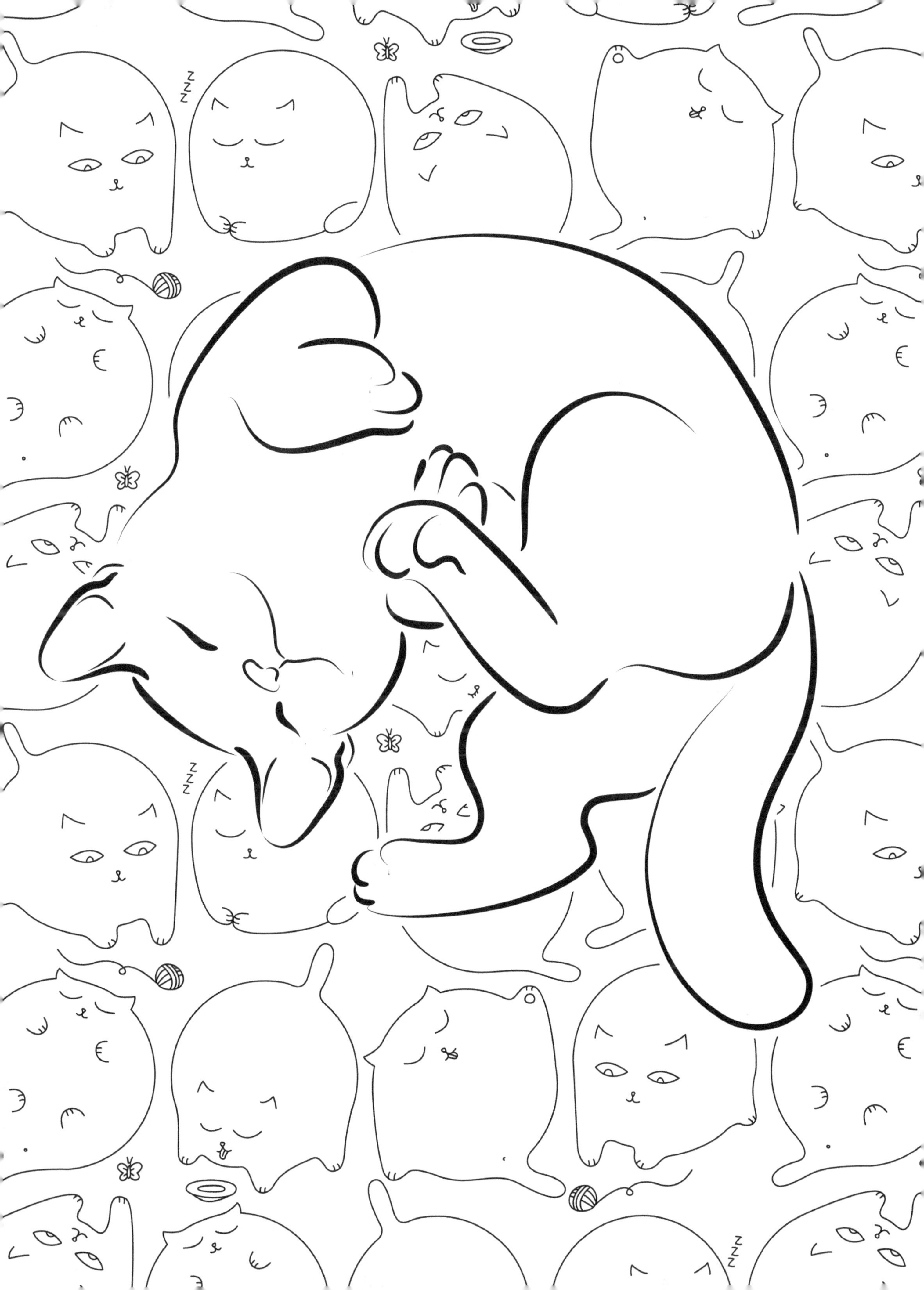

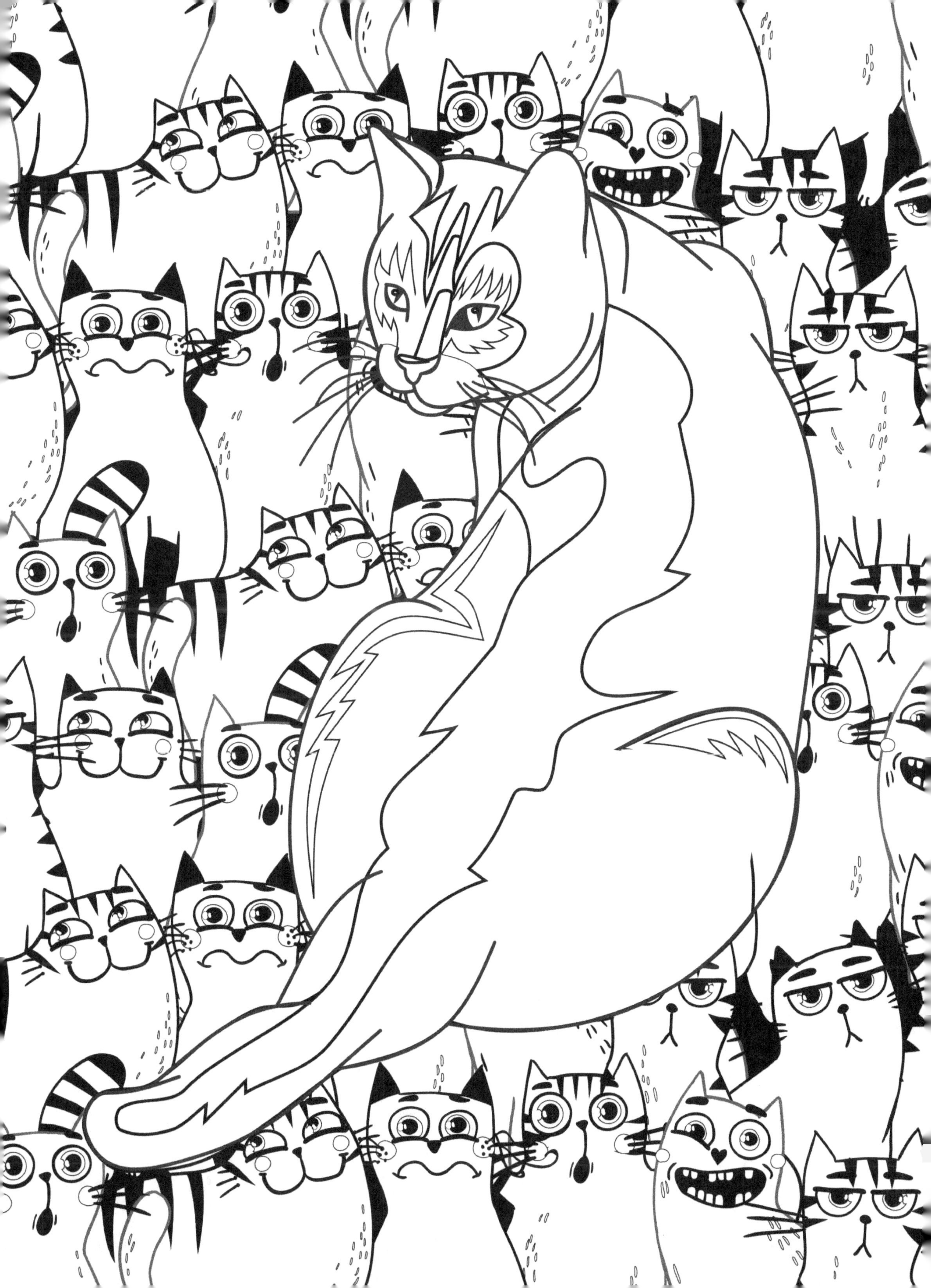

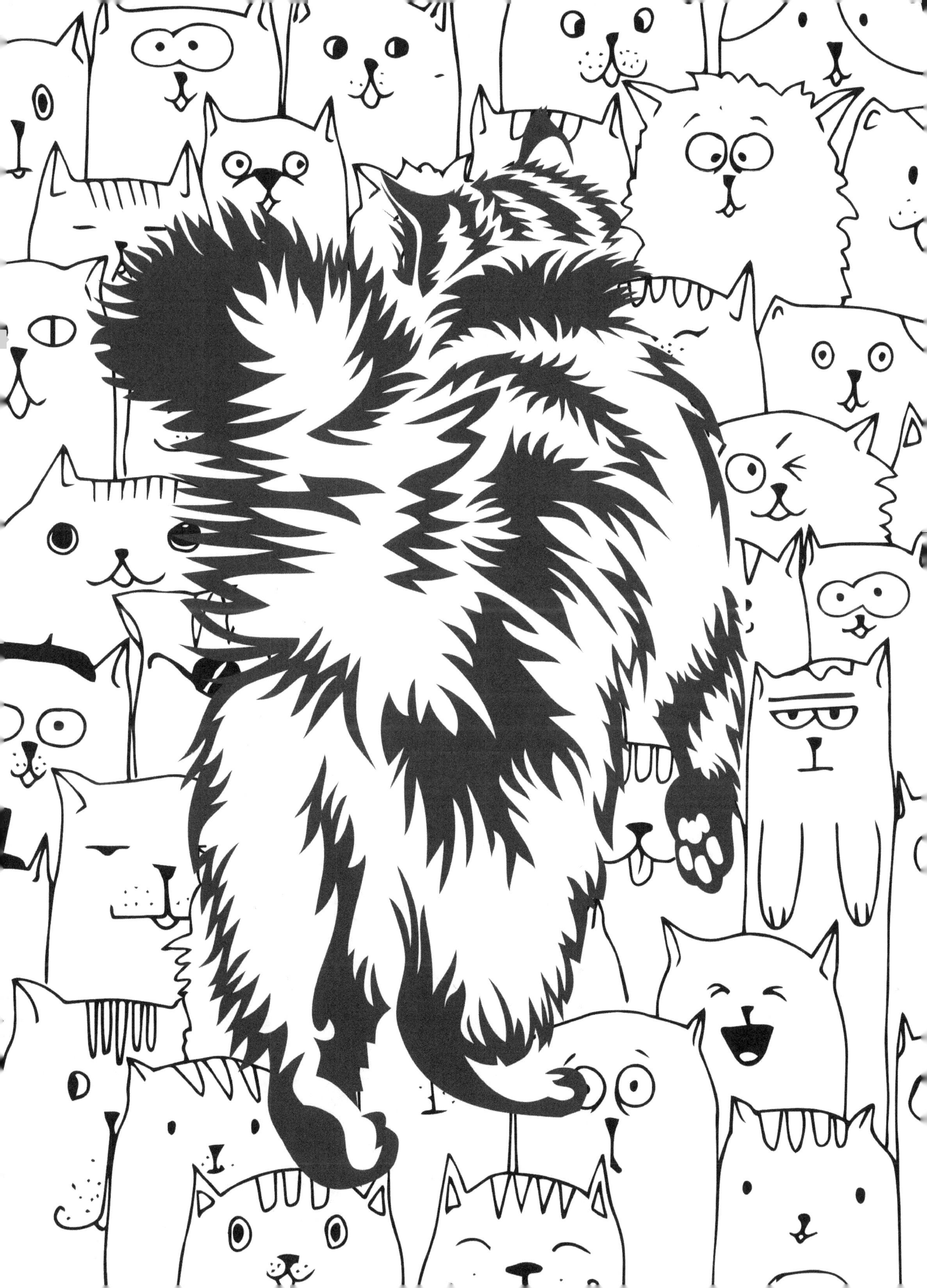

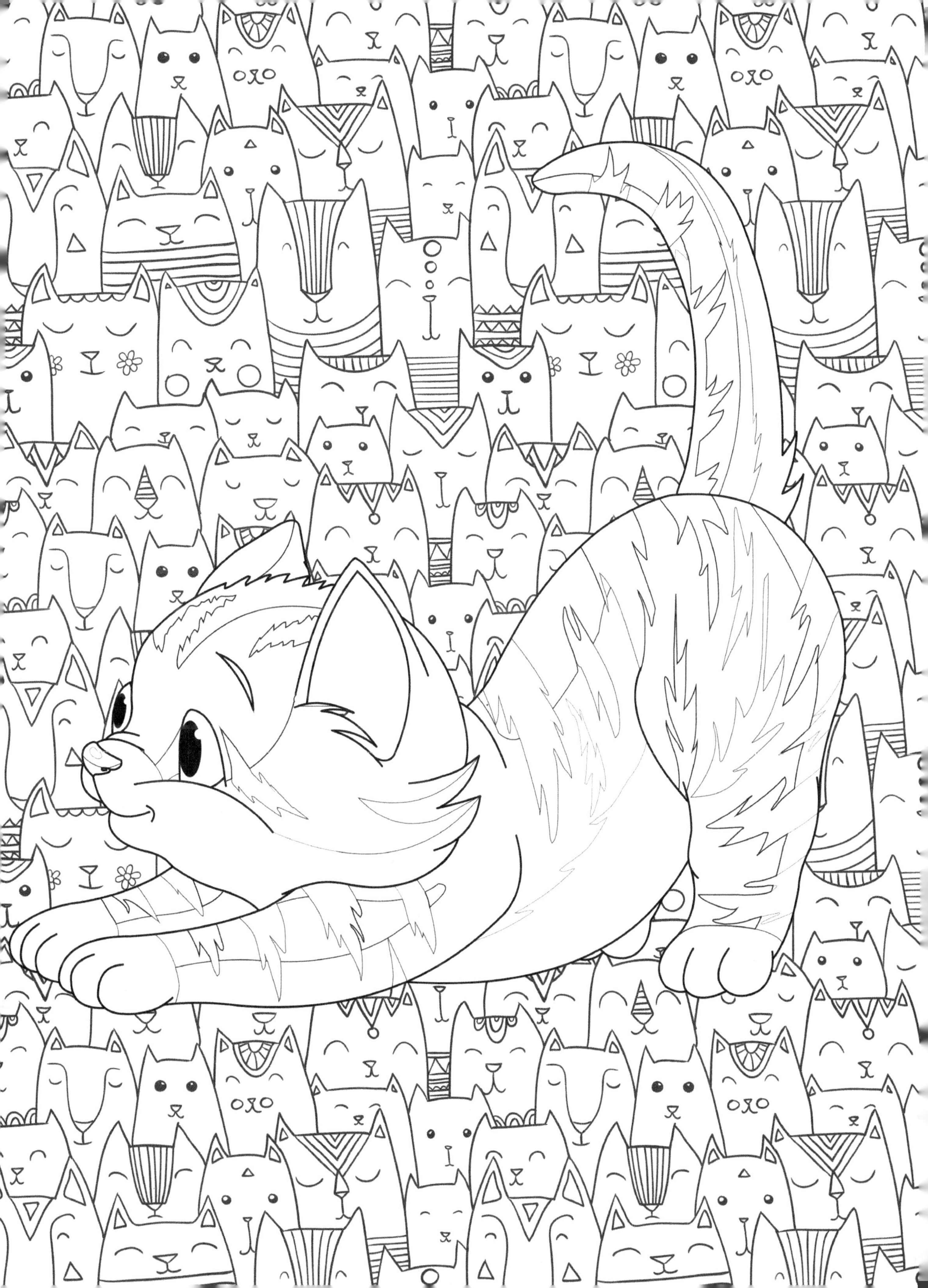

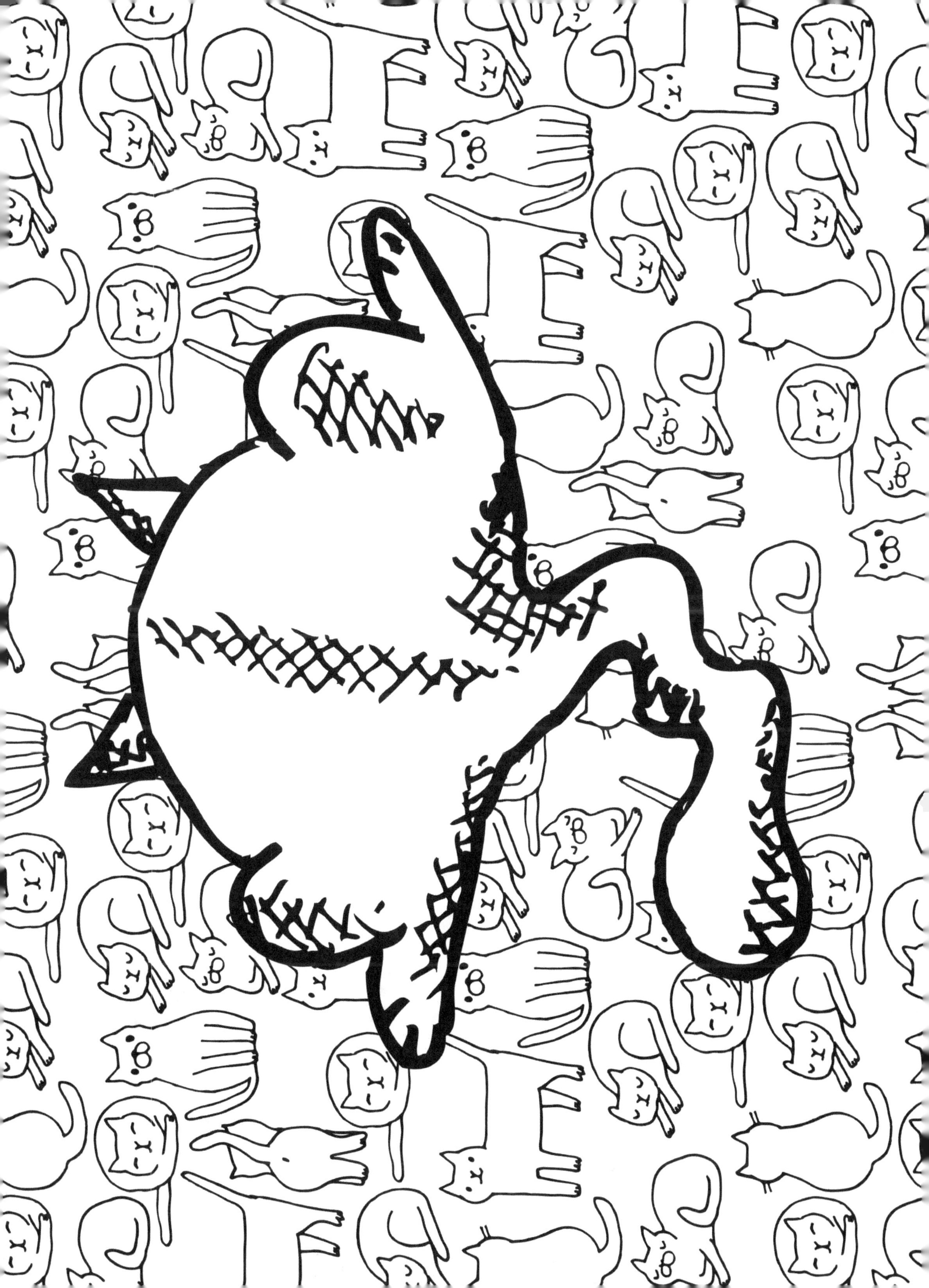

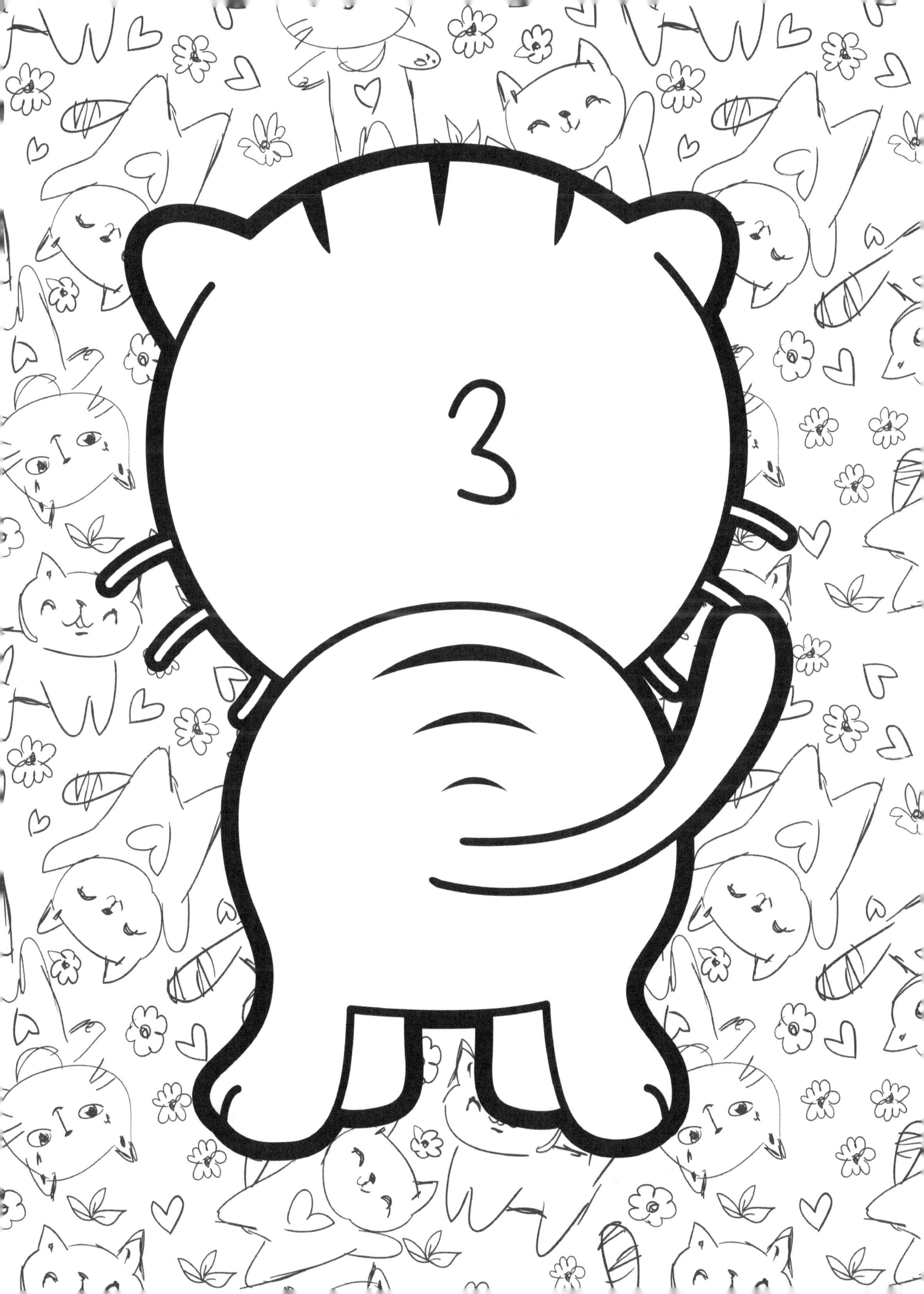
3

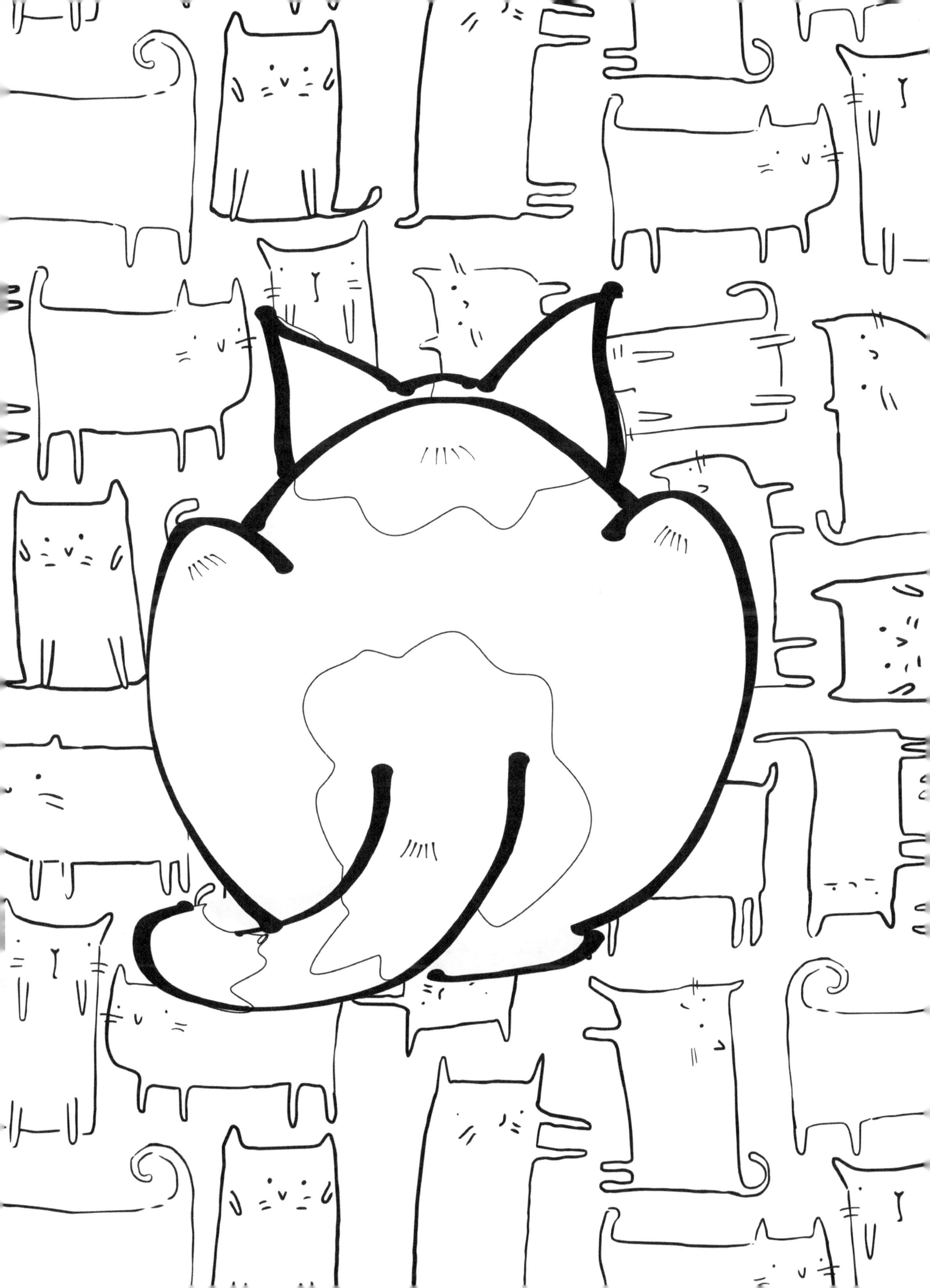

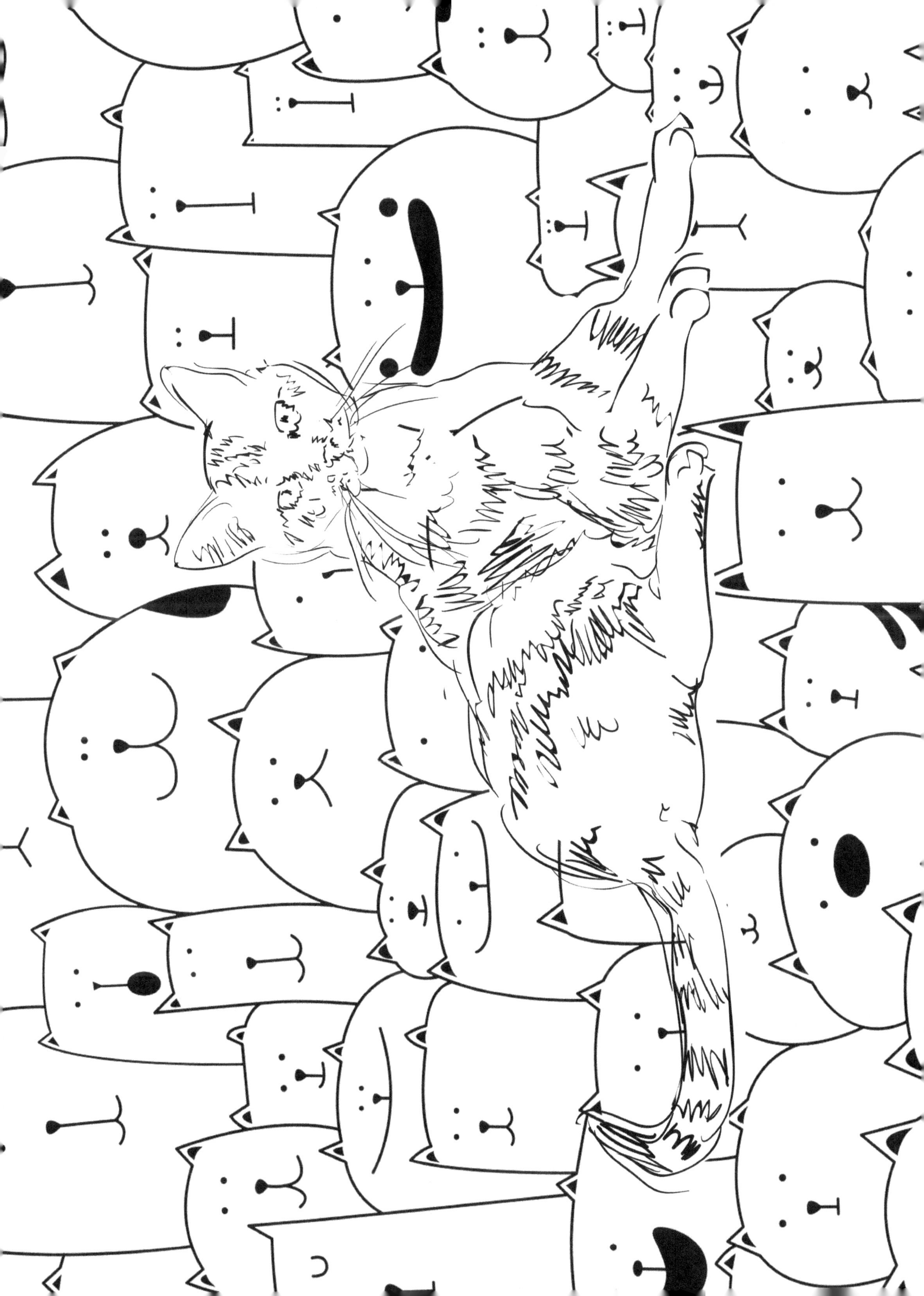

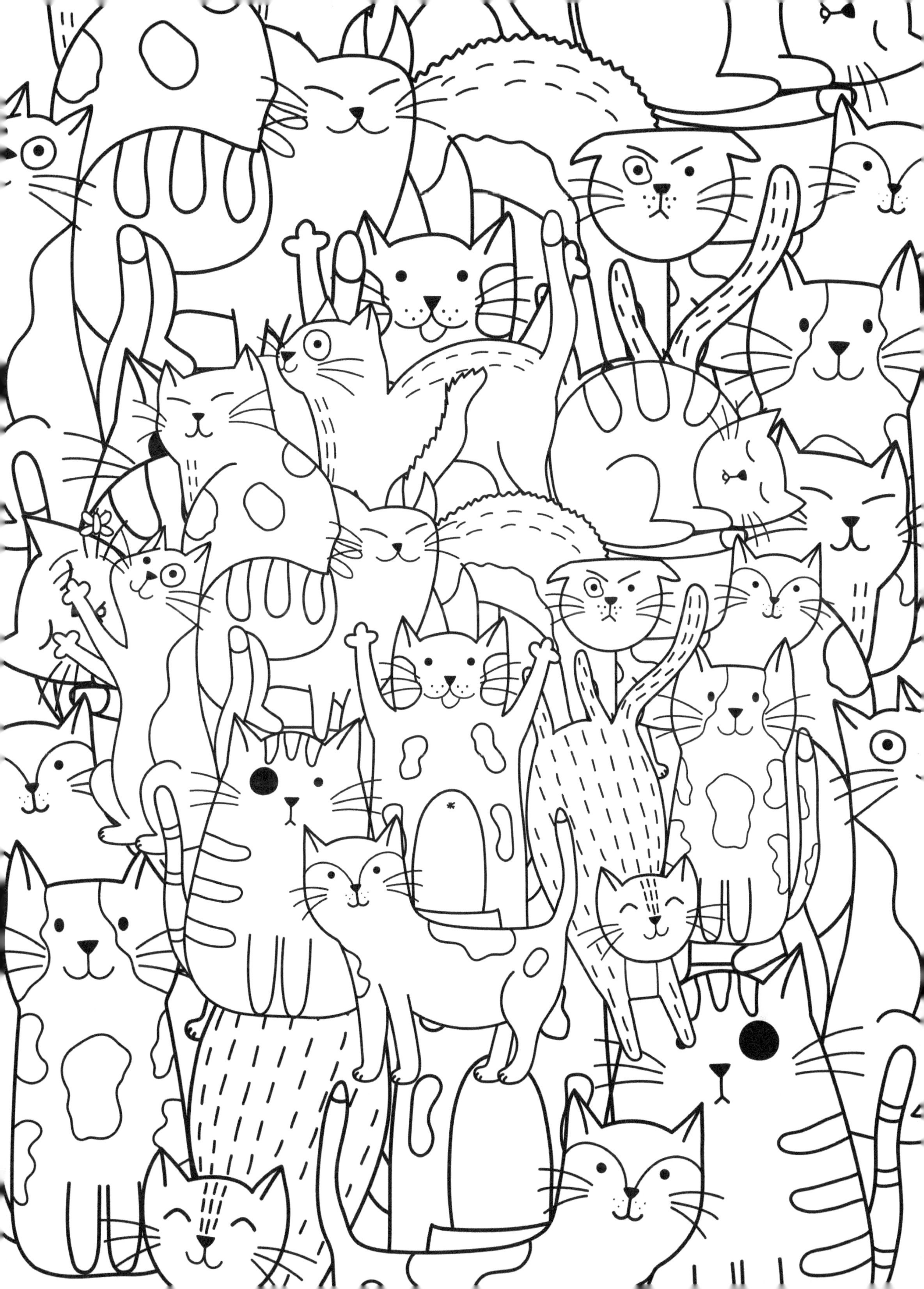

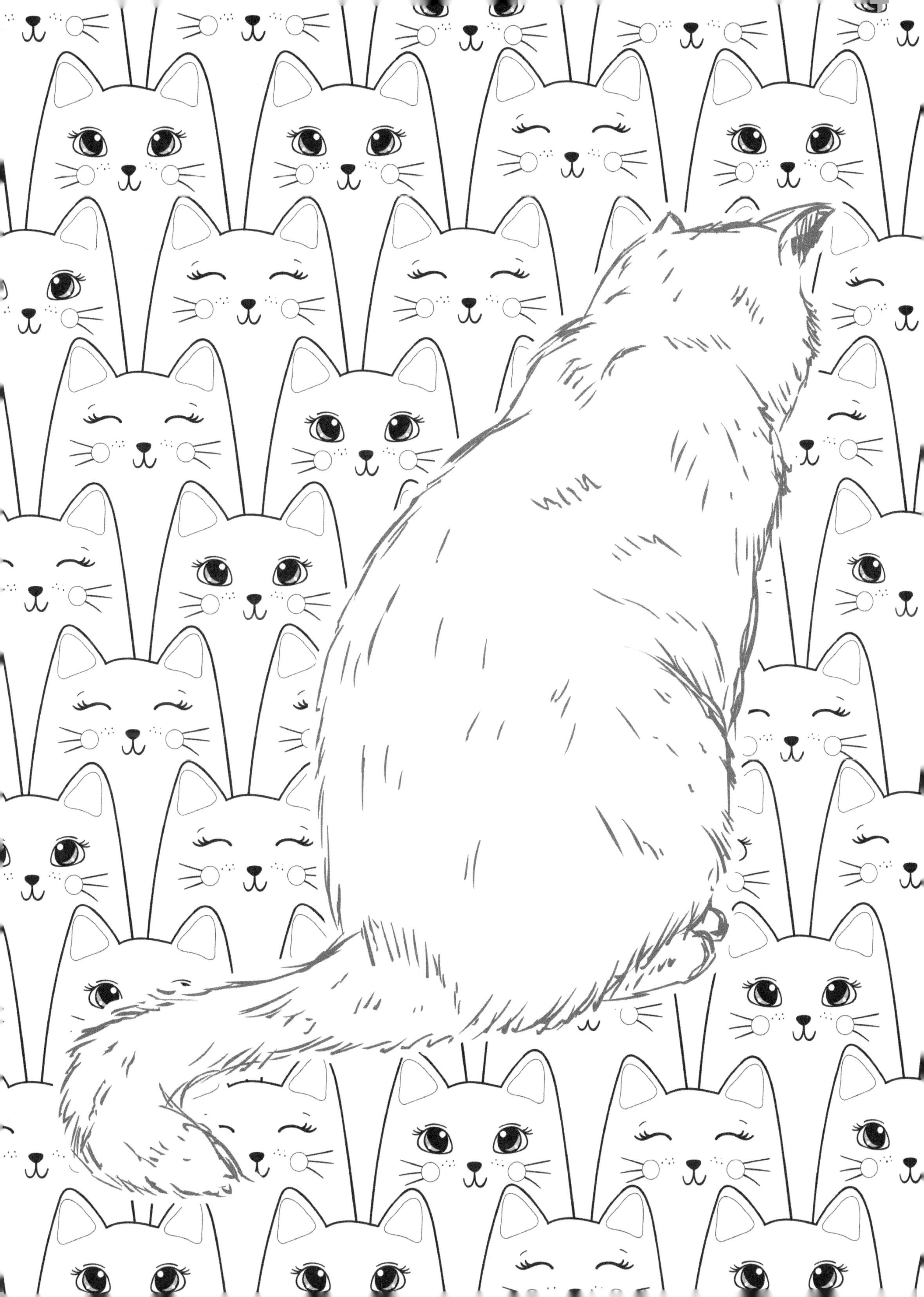

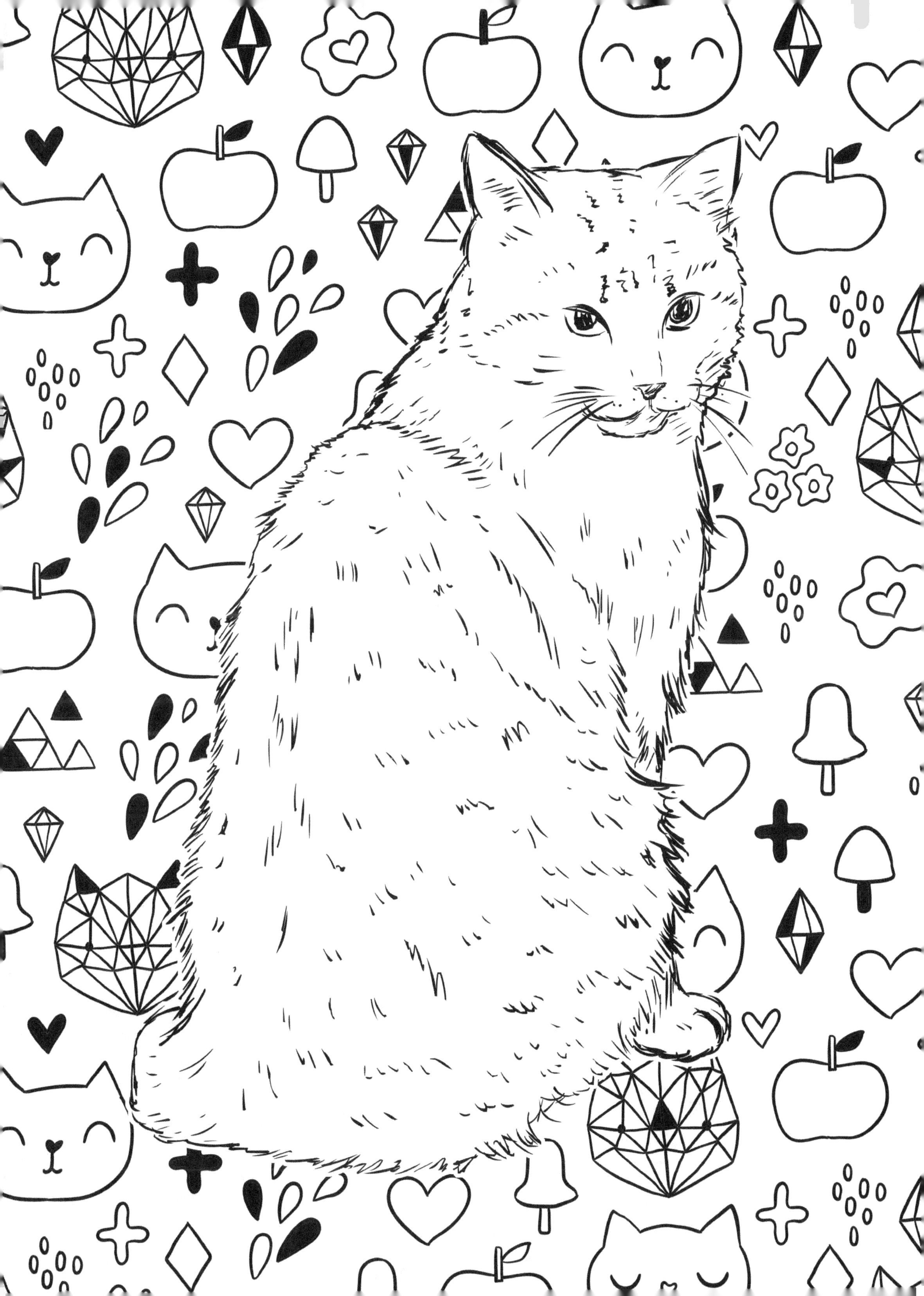

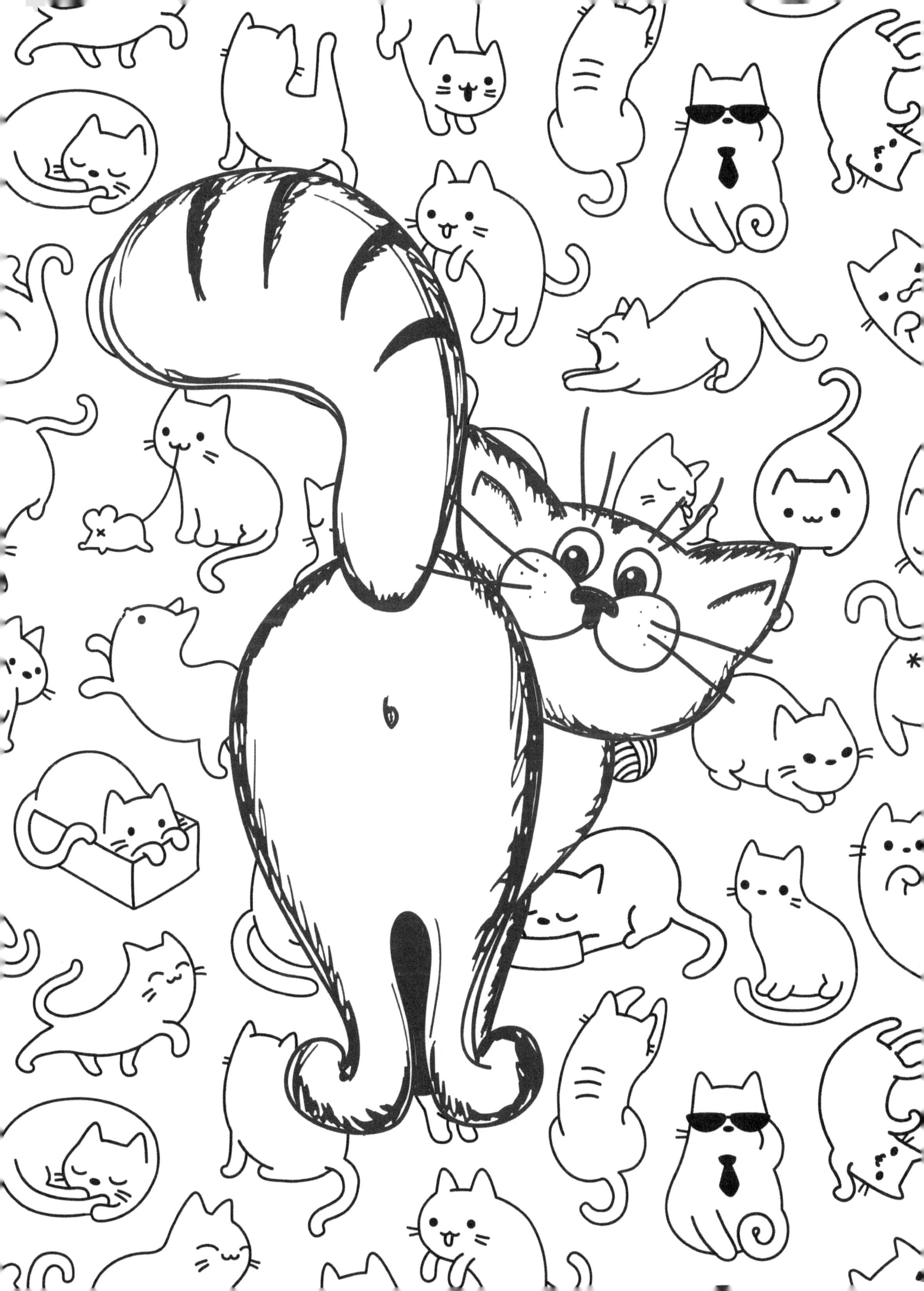

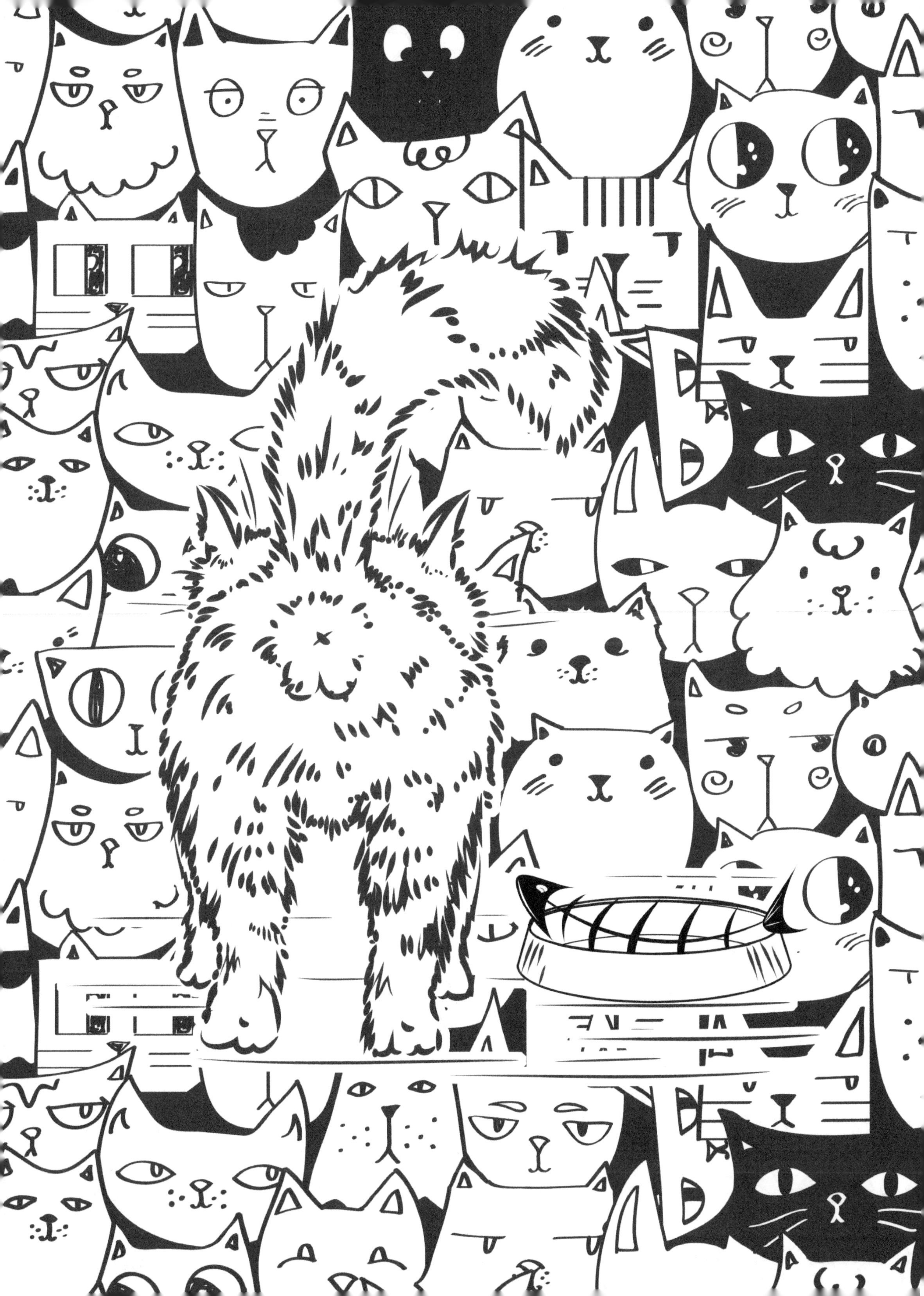

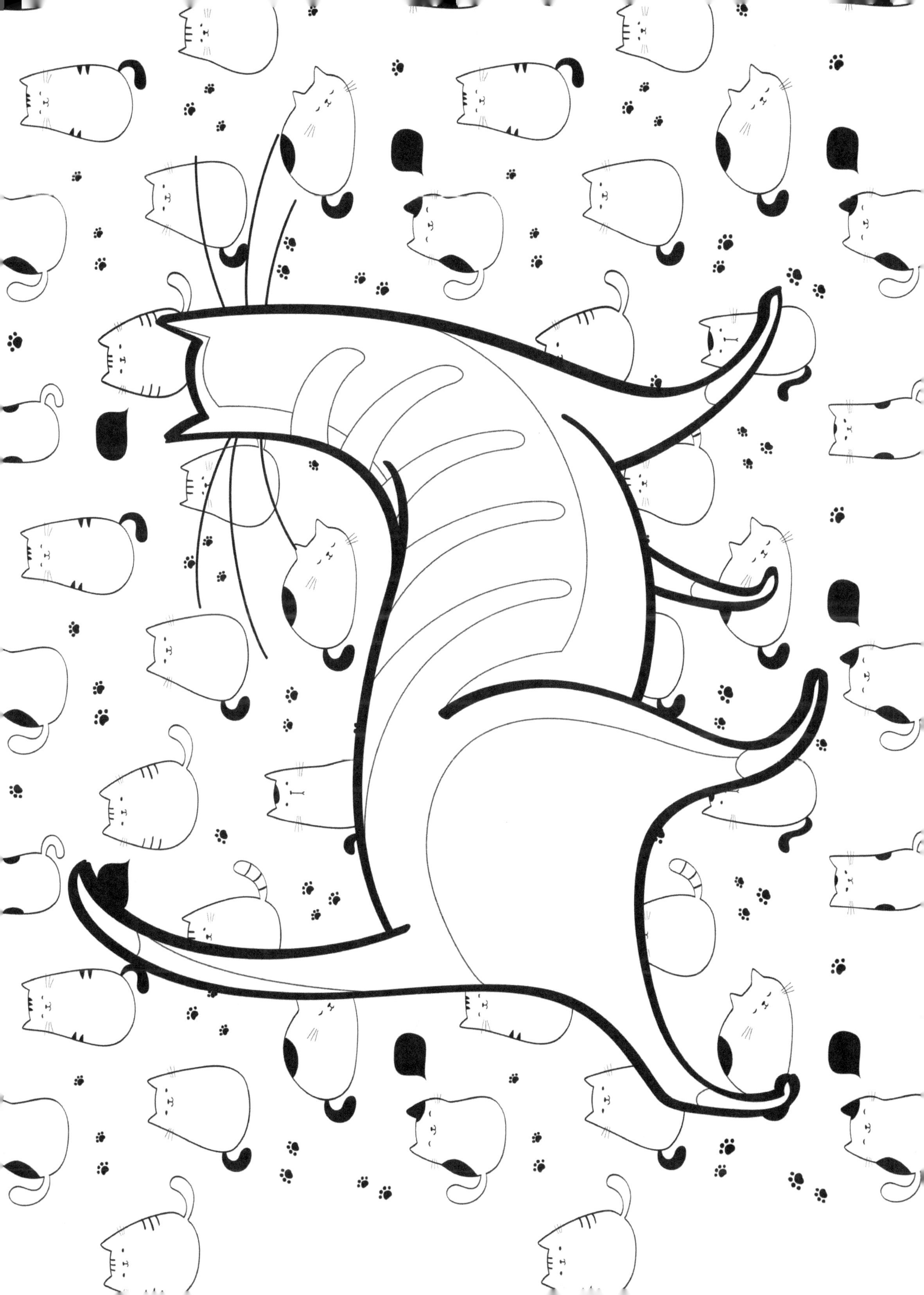

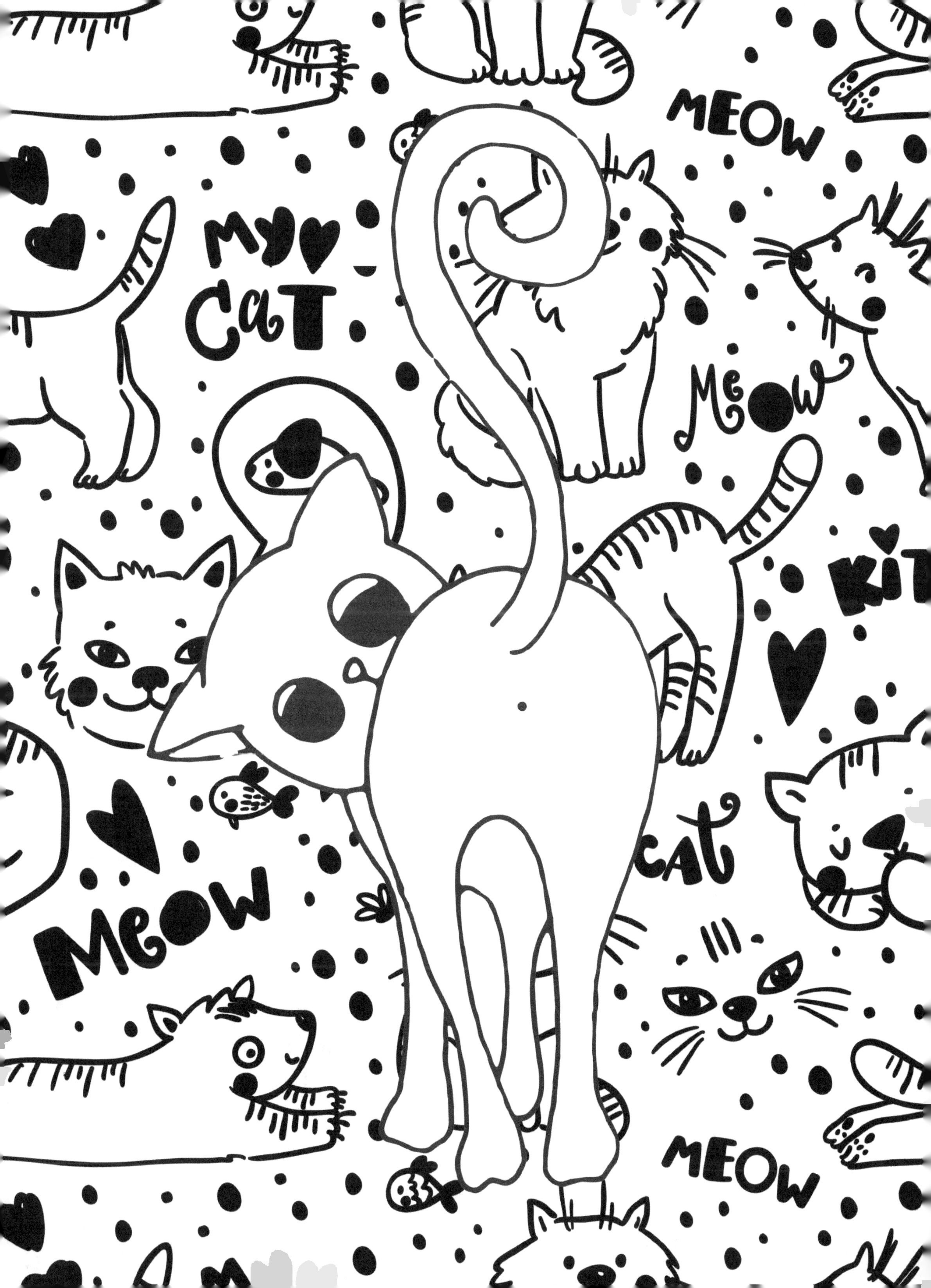
MEOW
MY CAT
MEOW
KIT
MEOW
CAT
MEOW

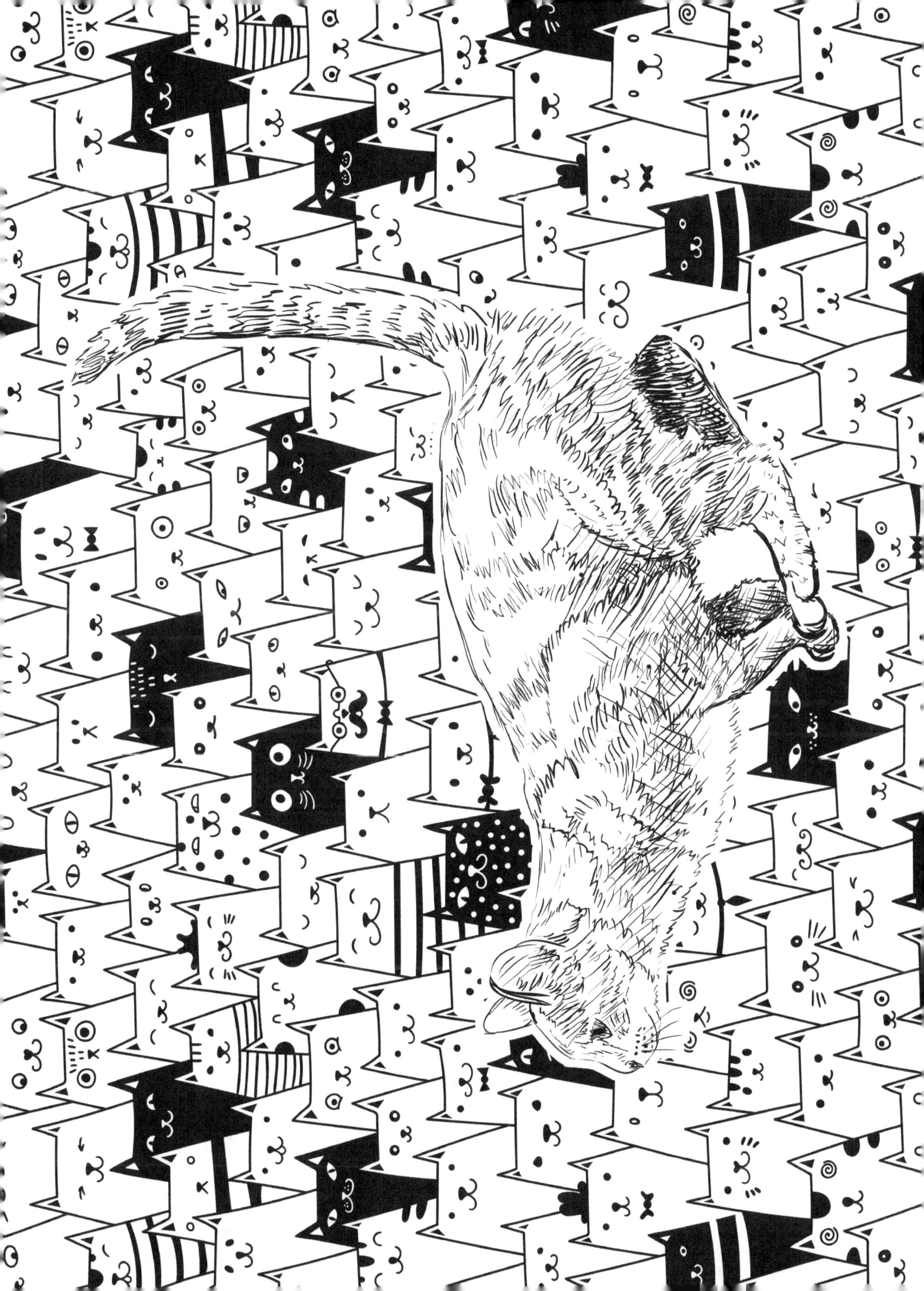

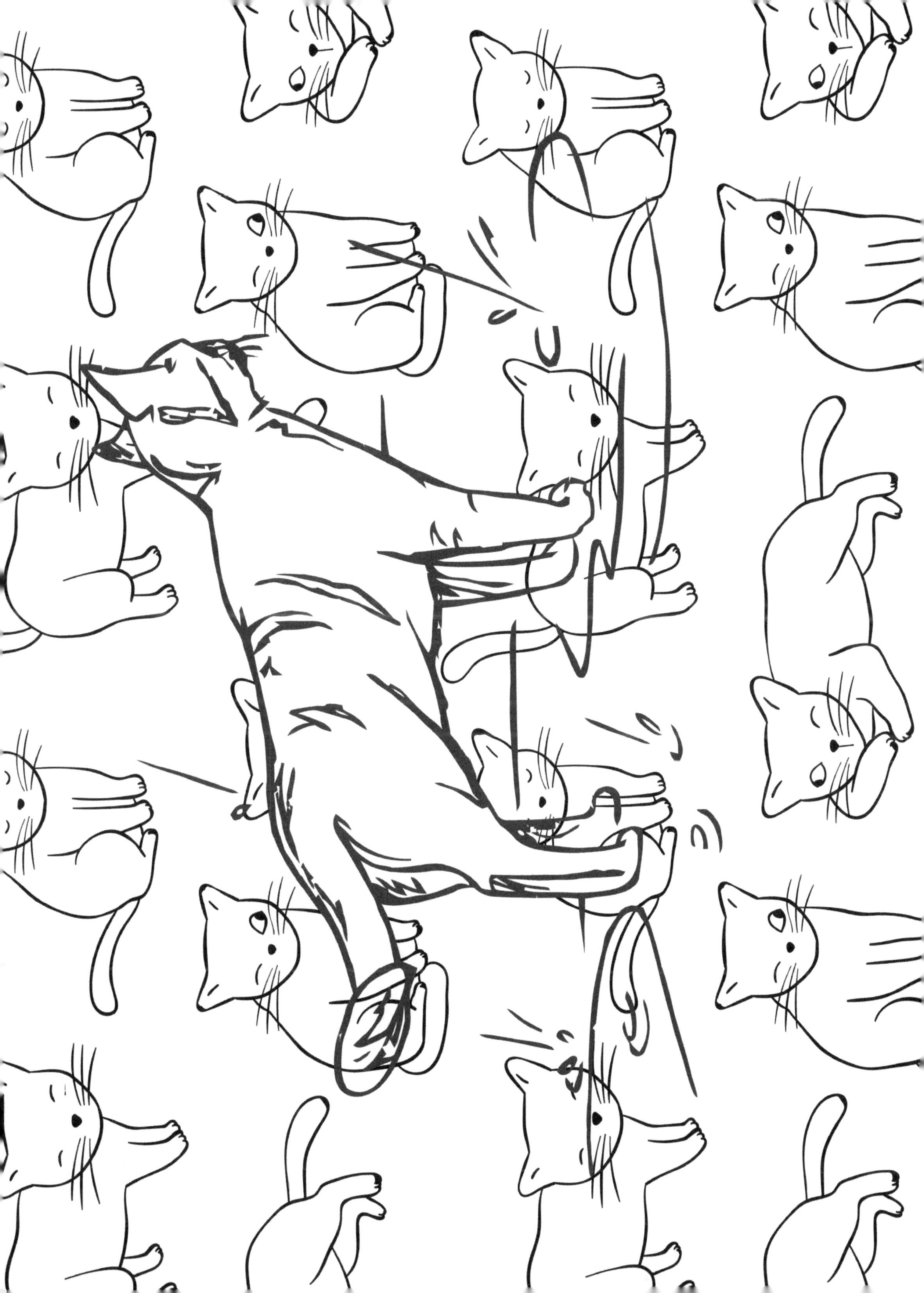

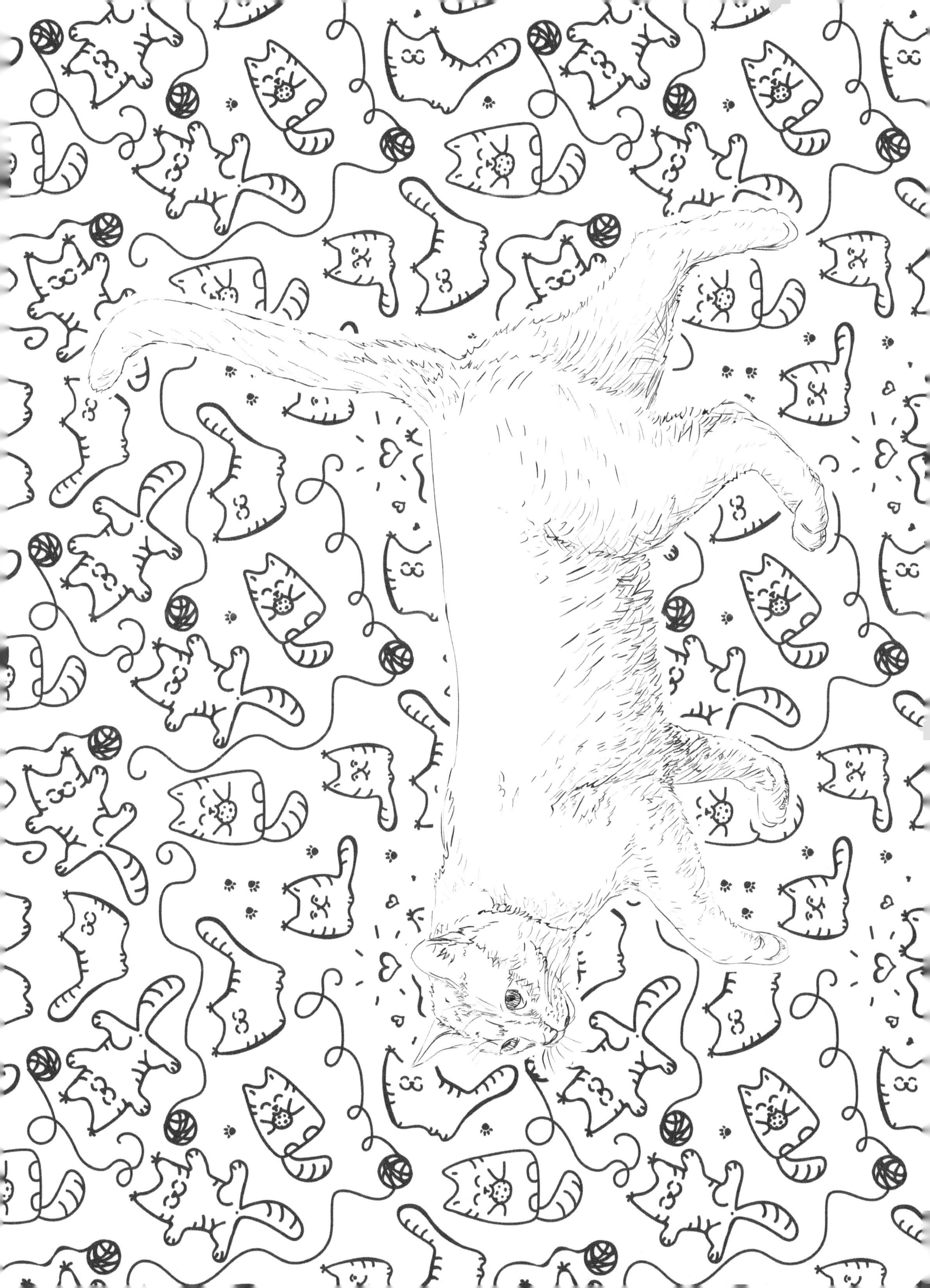

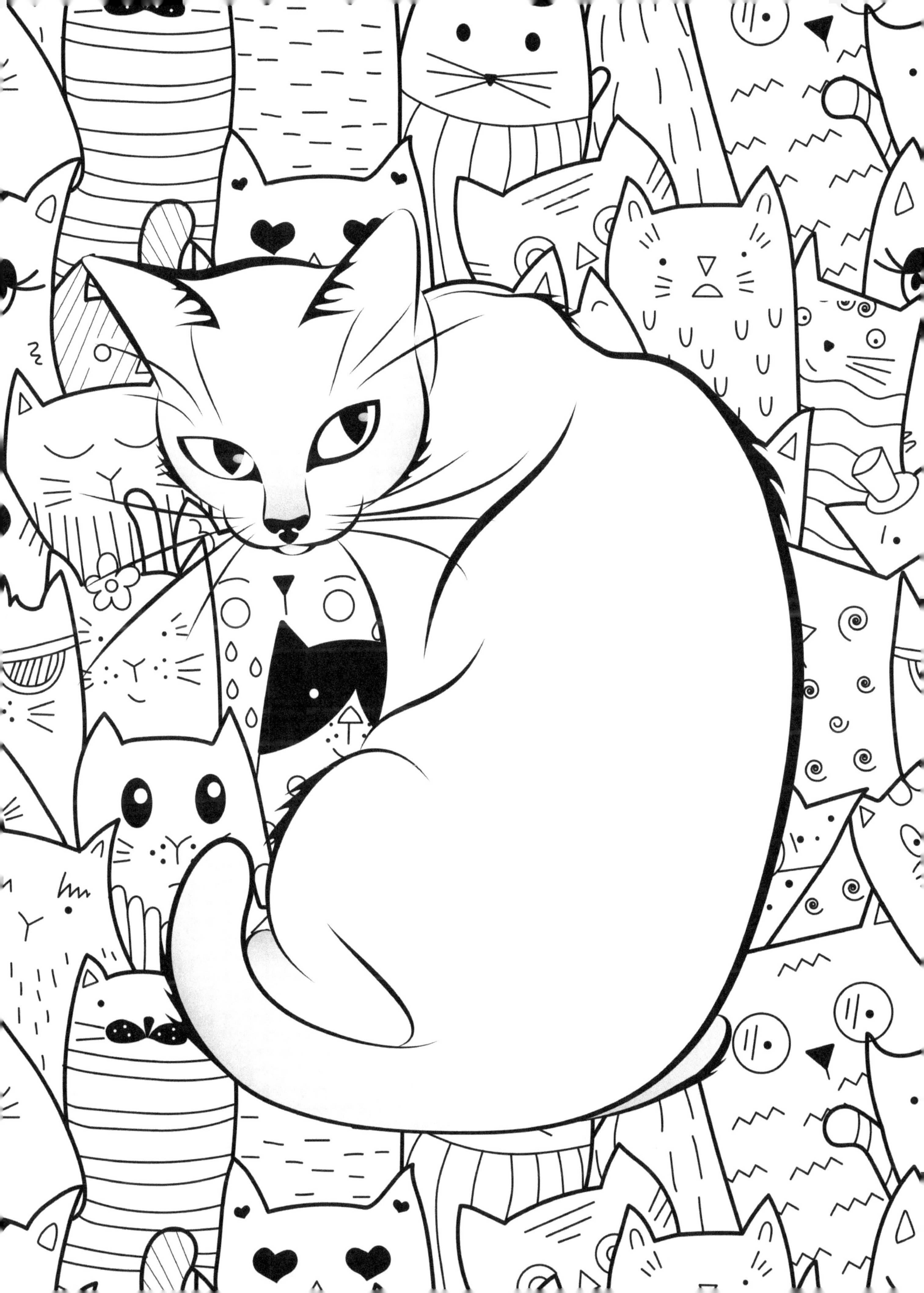

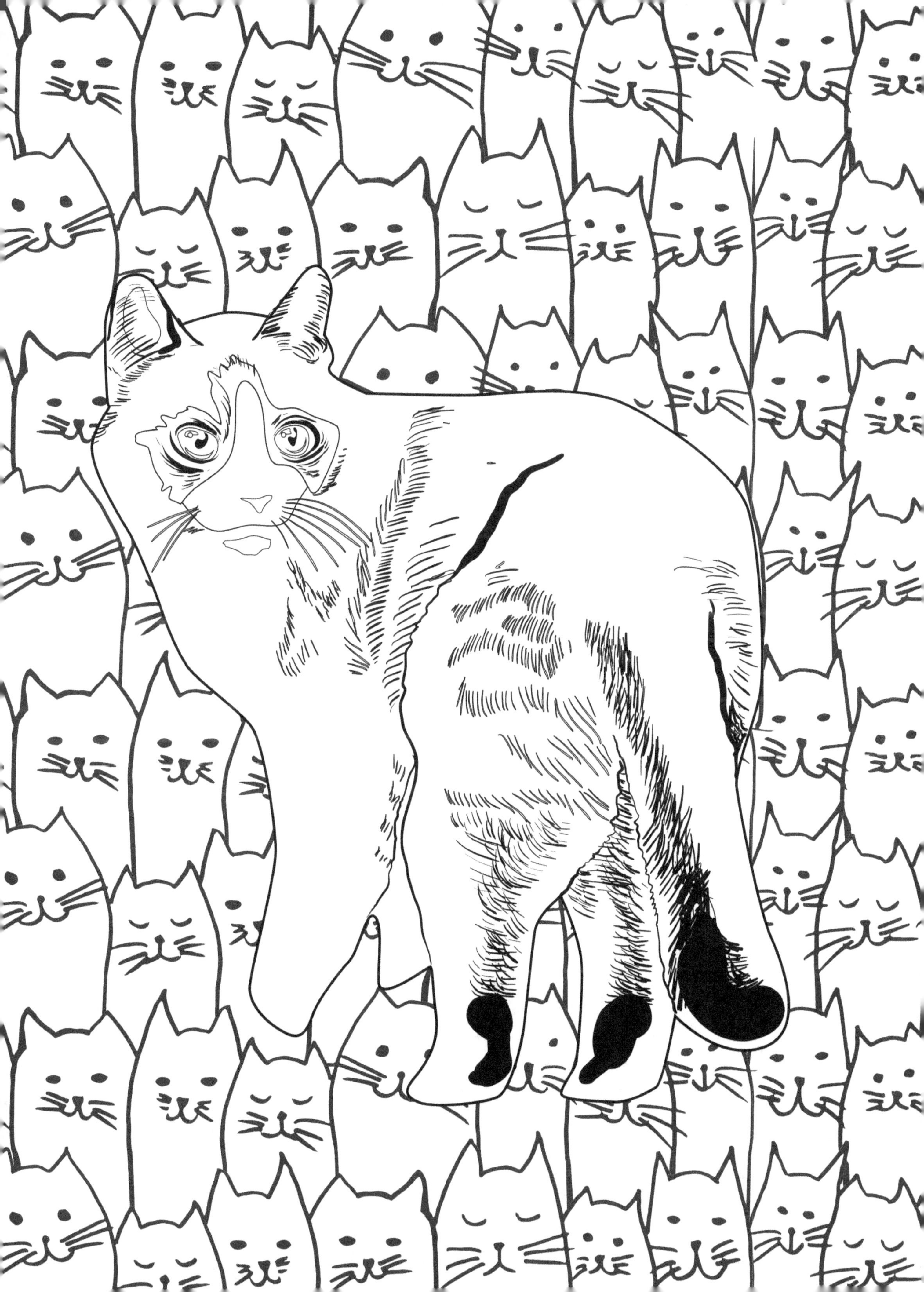

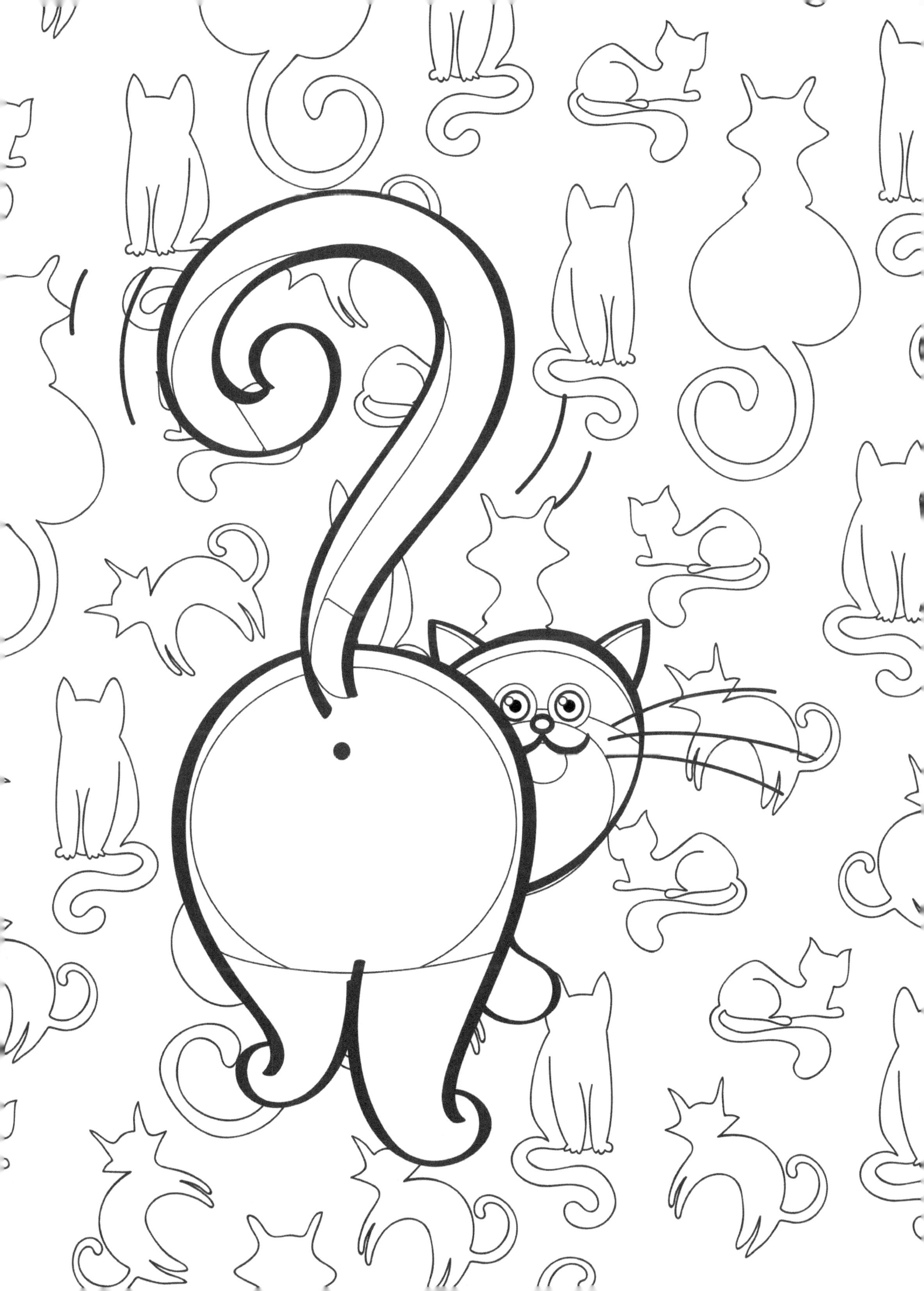

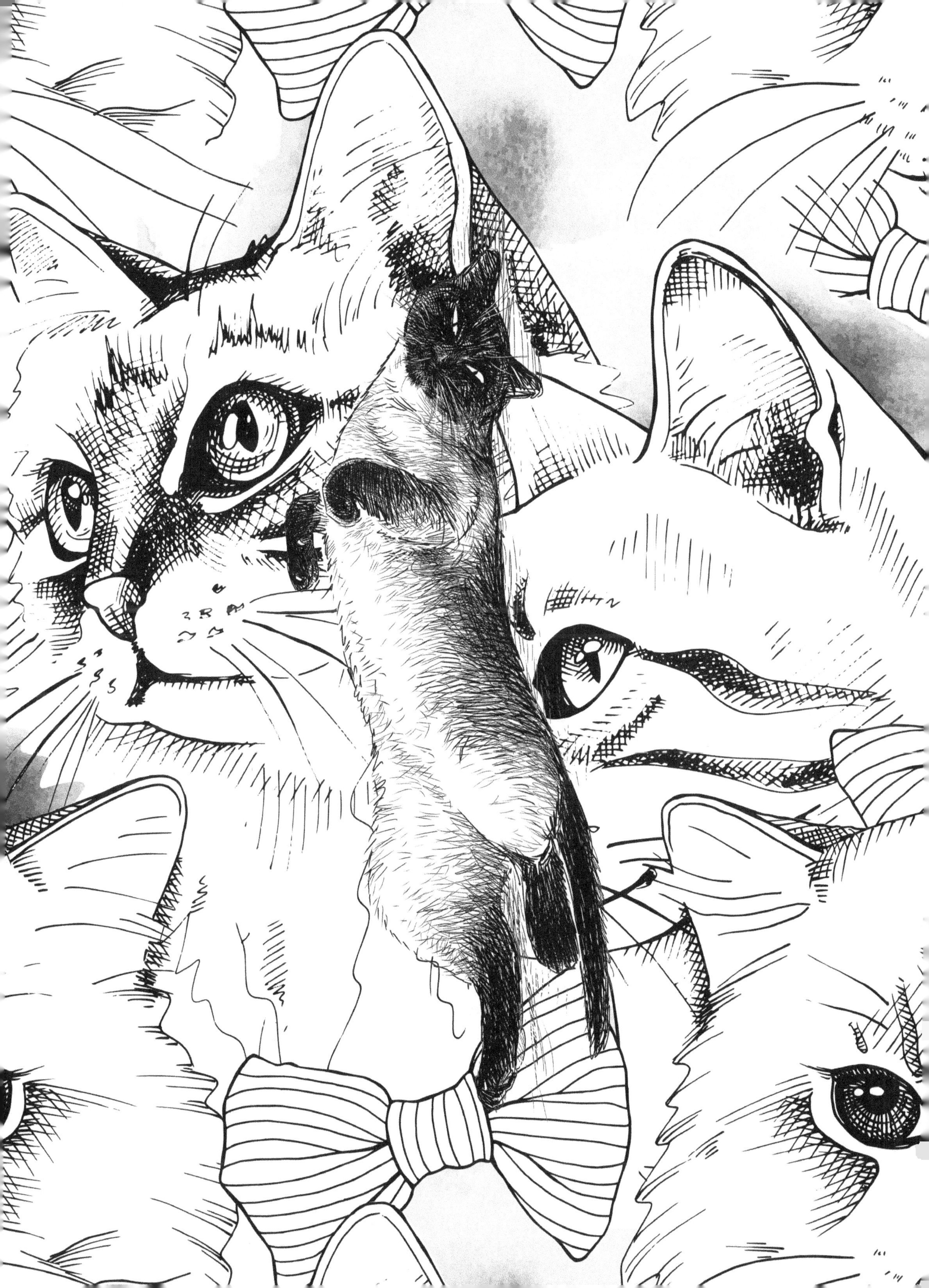

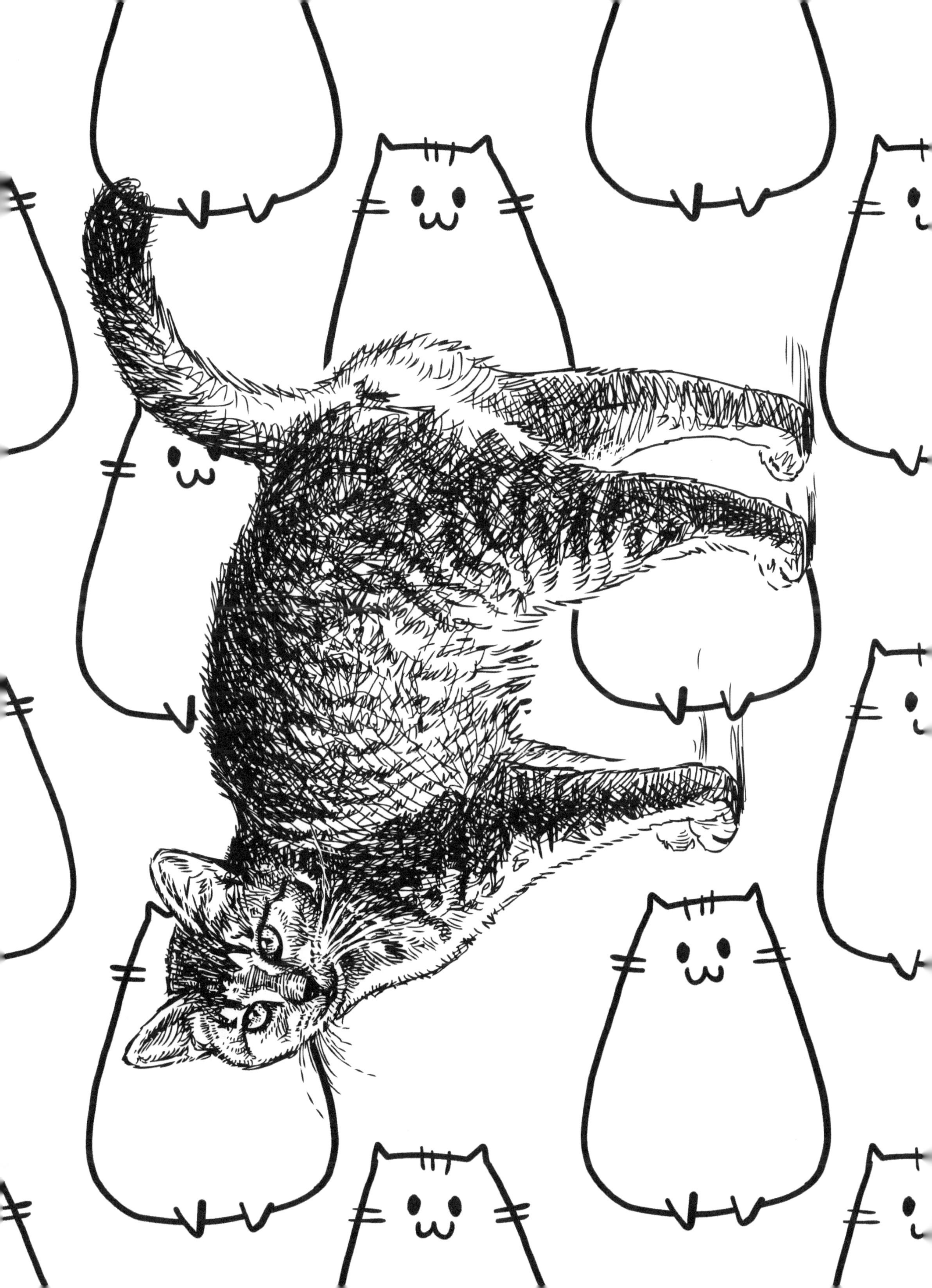

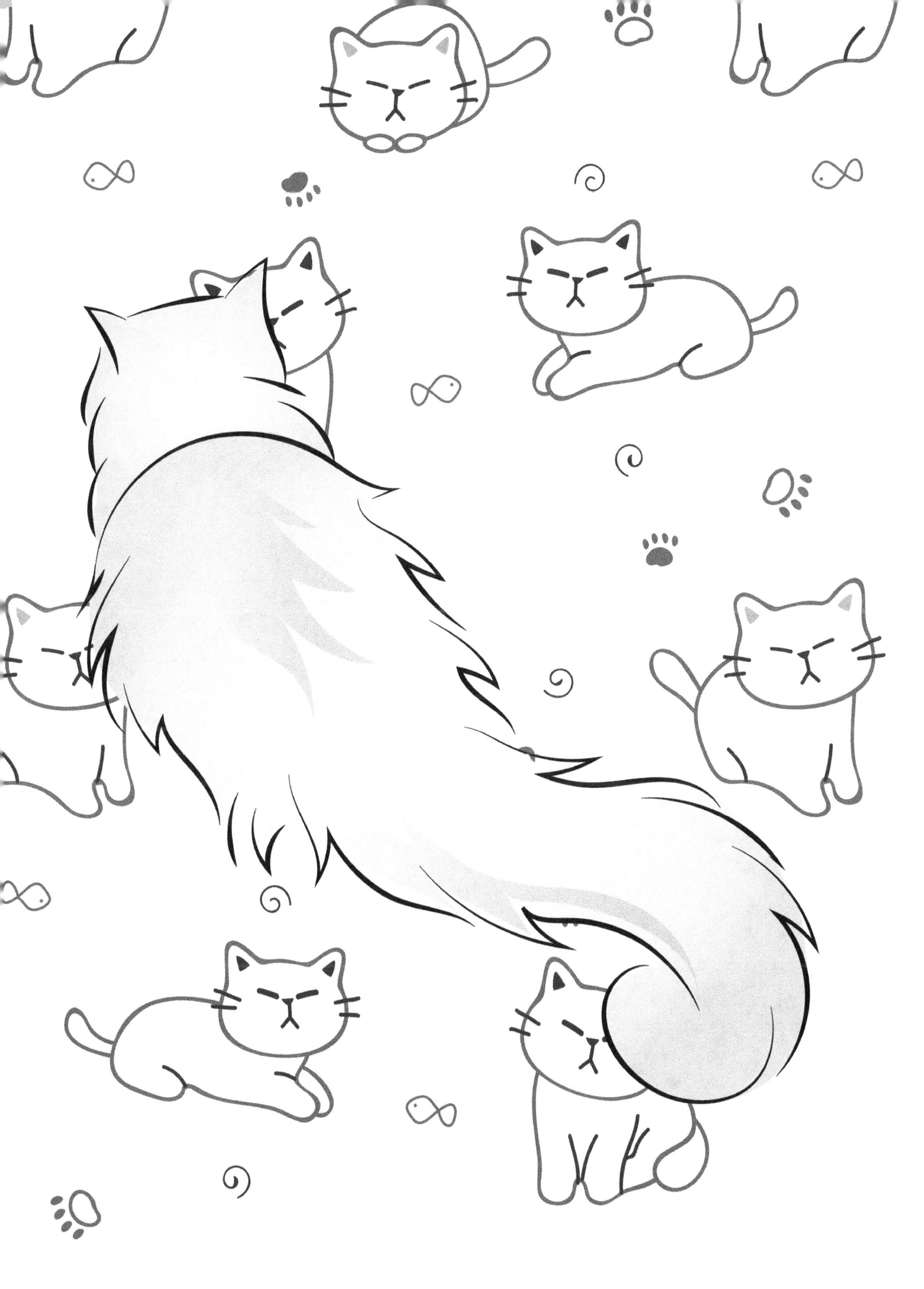

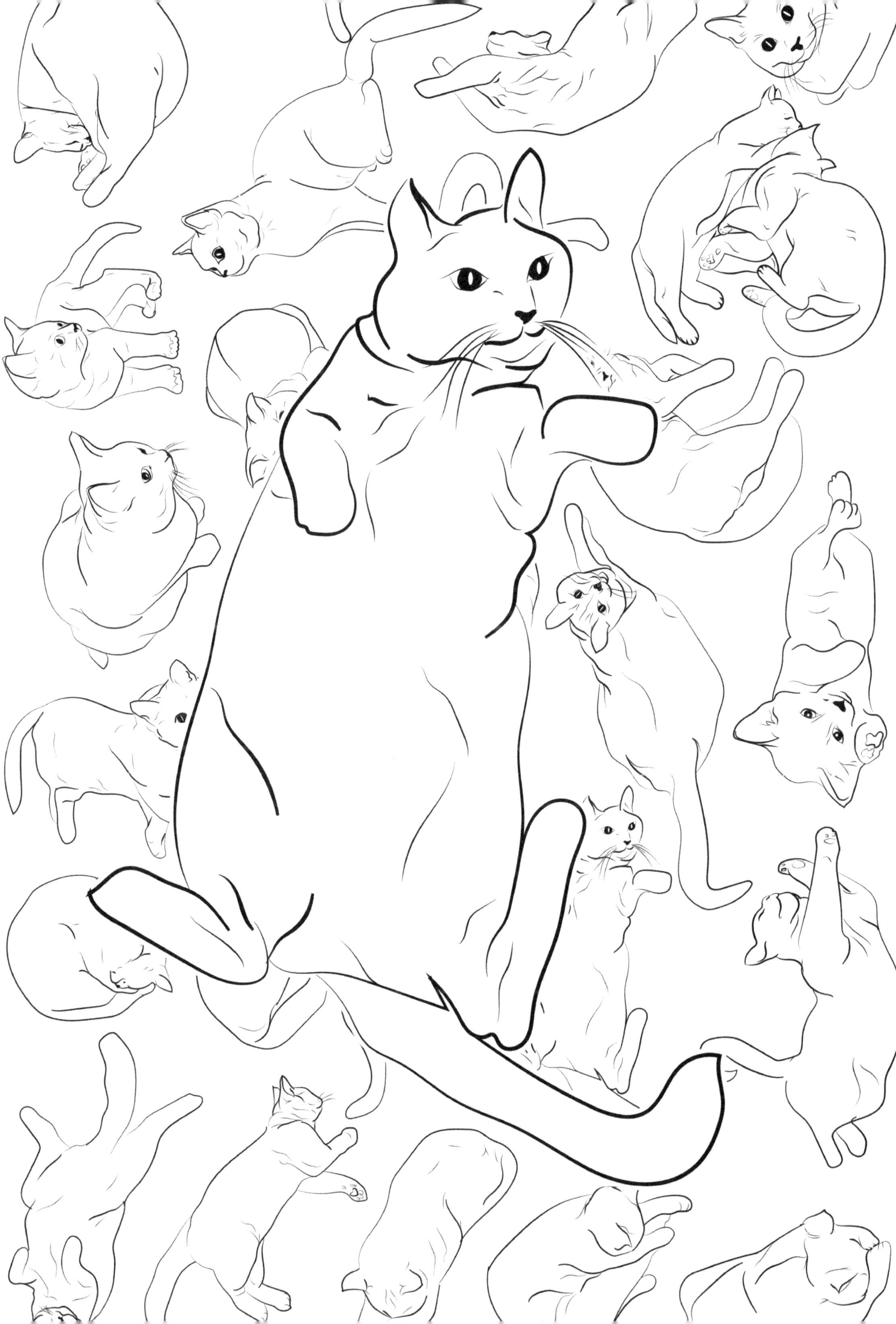

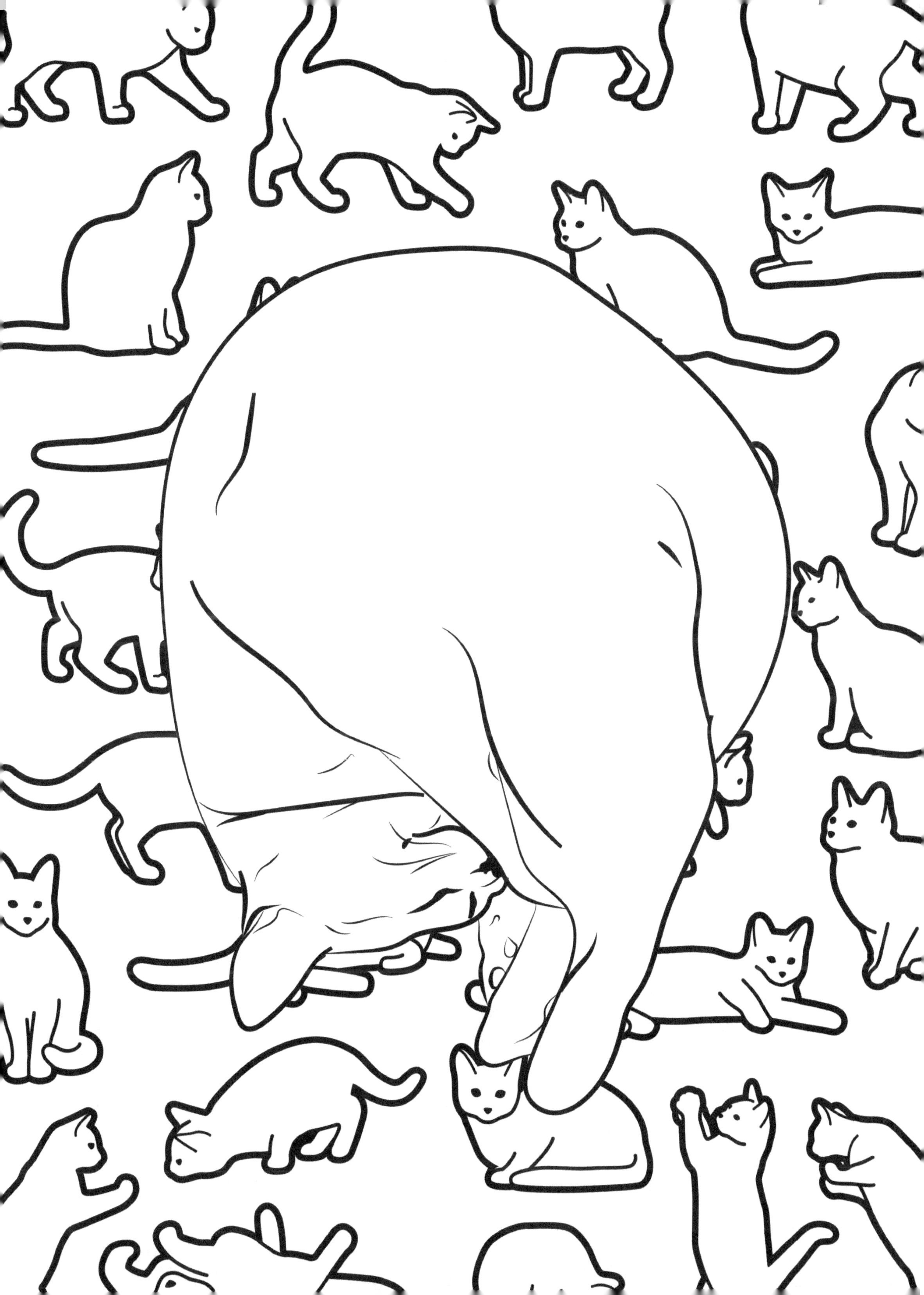

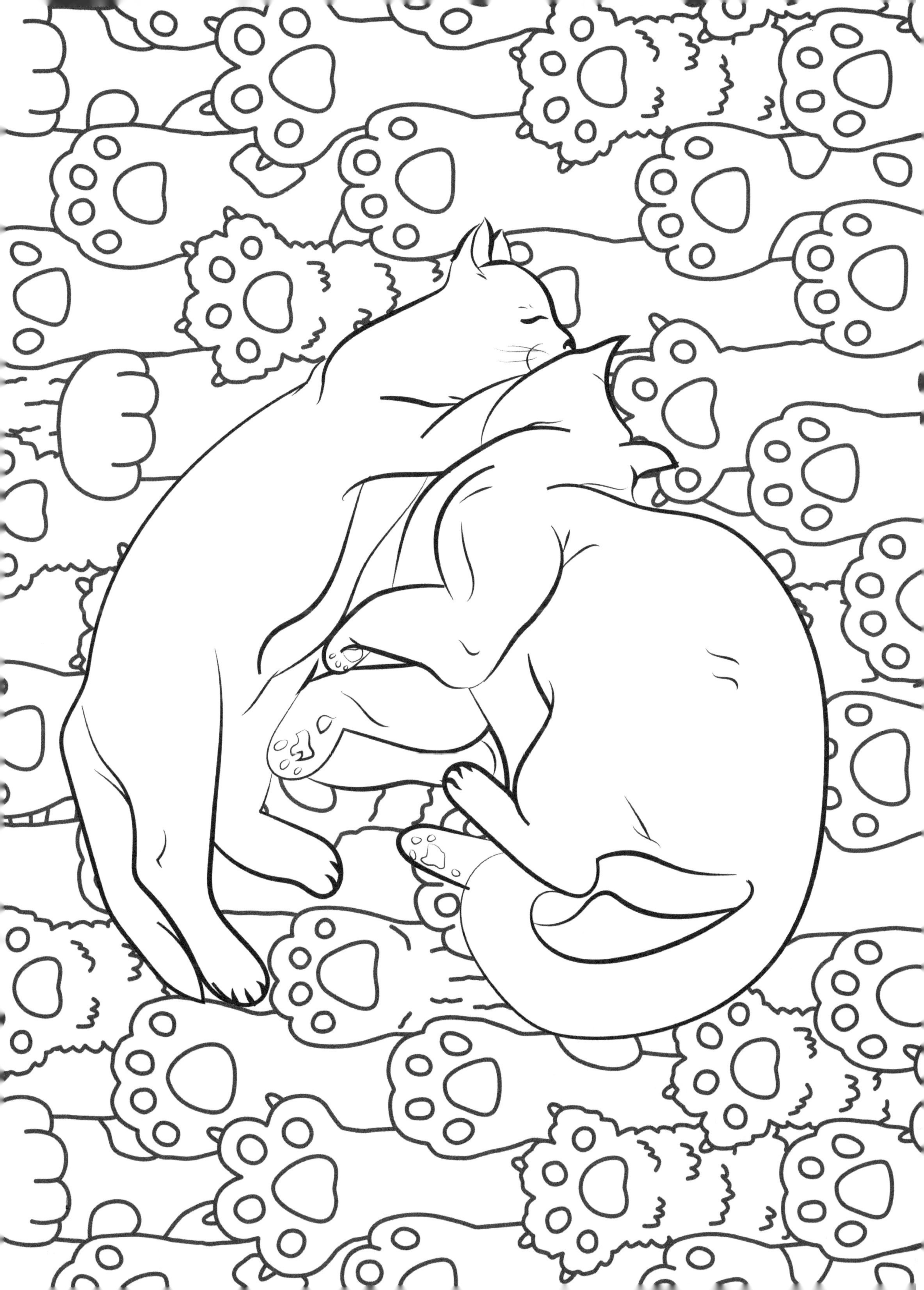

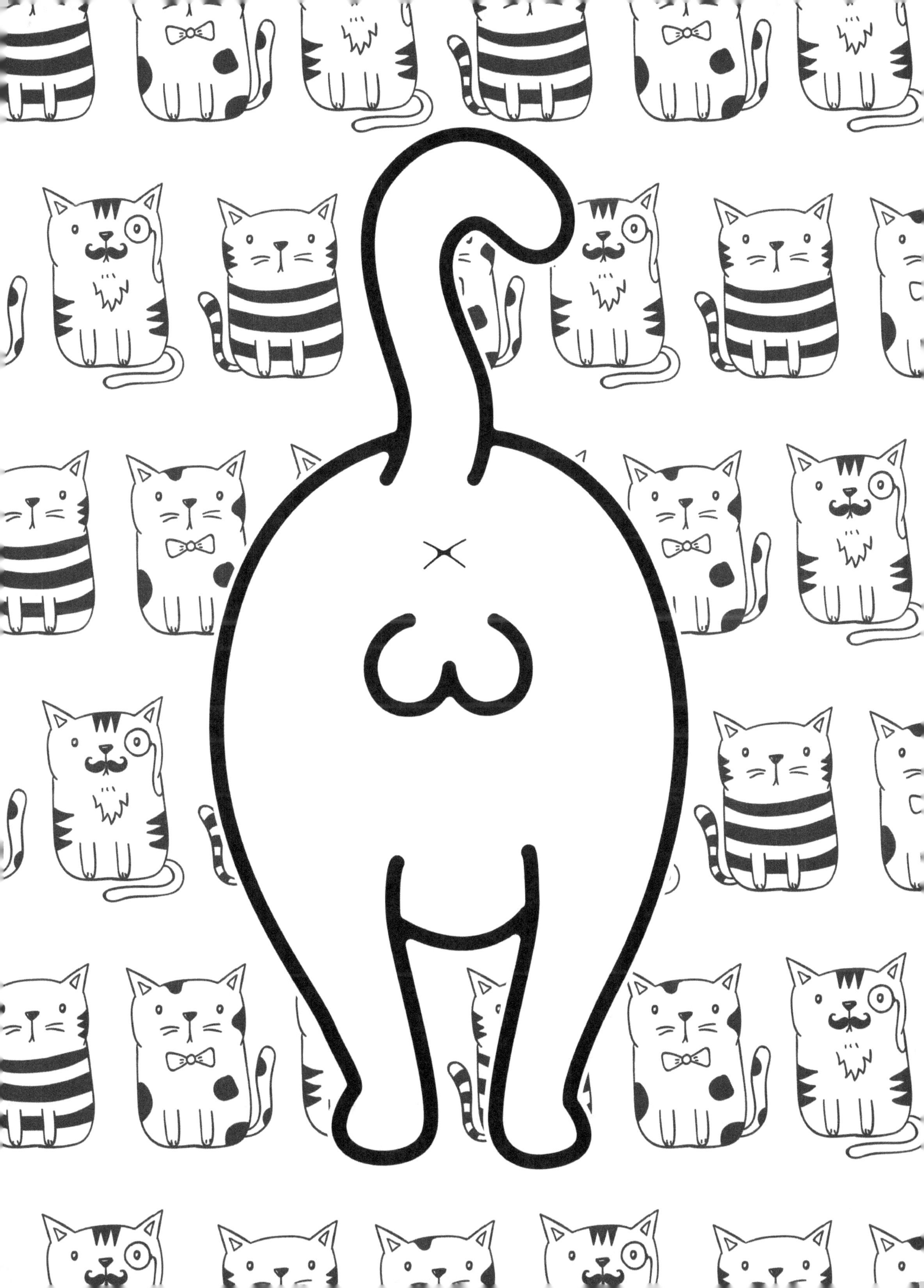

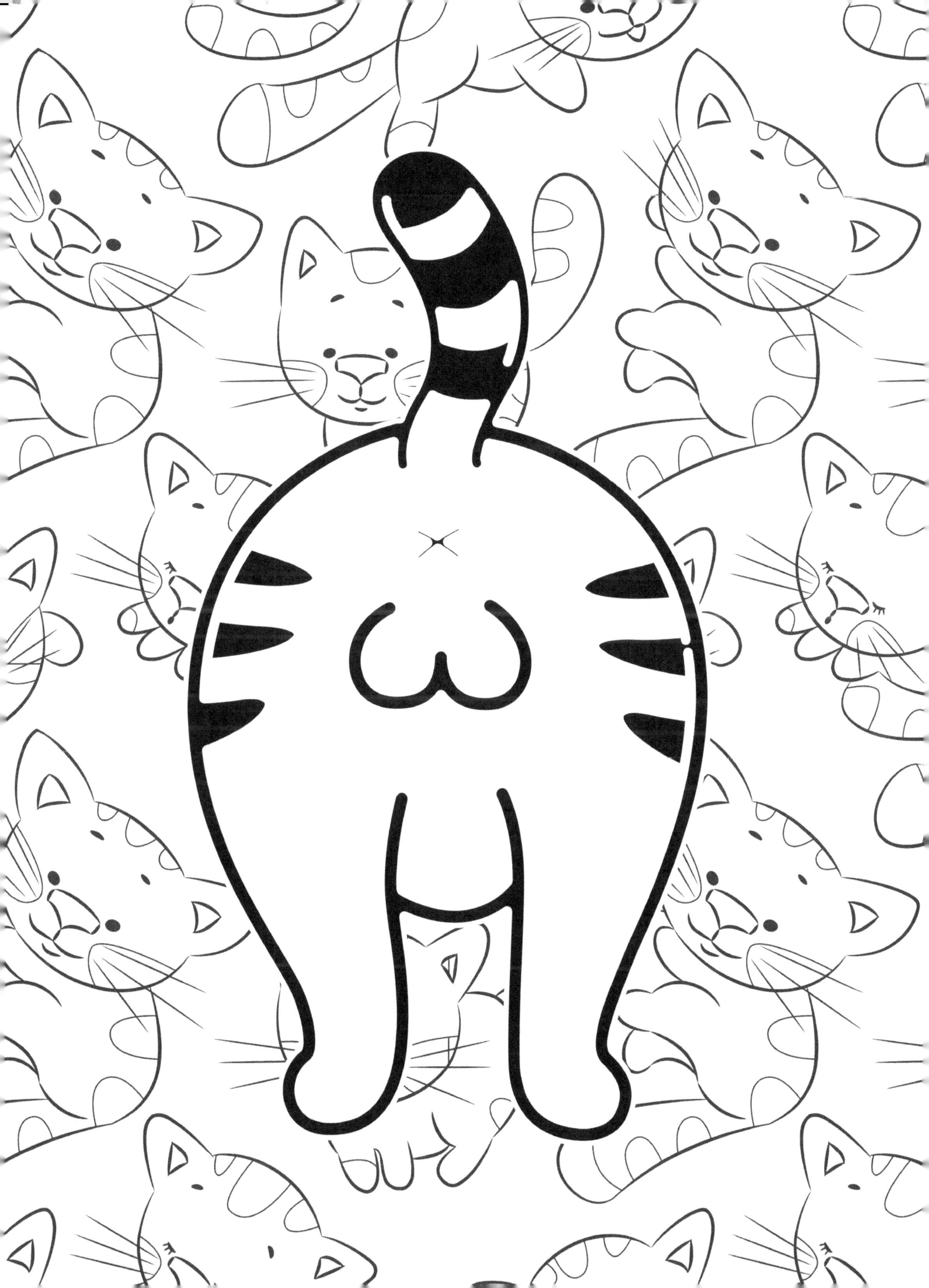

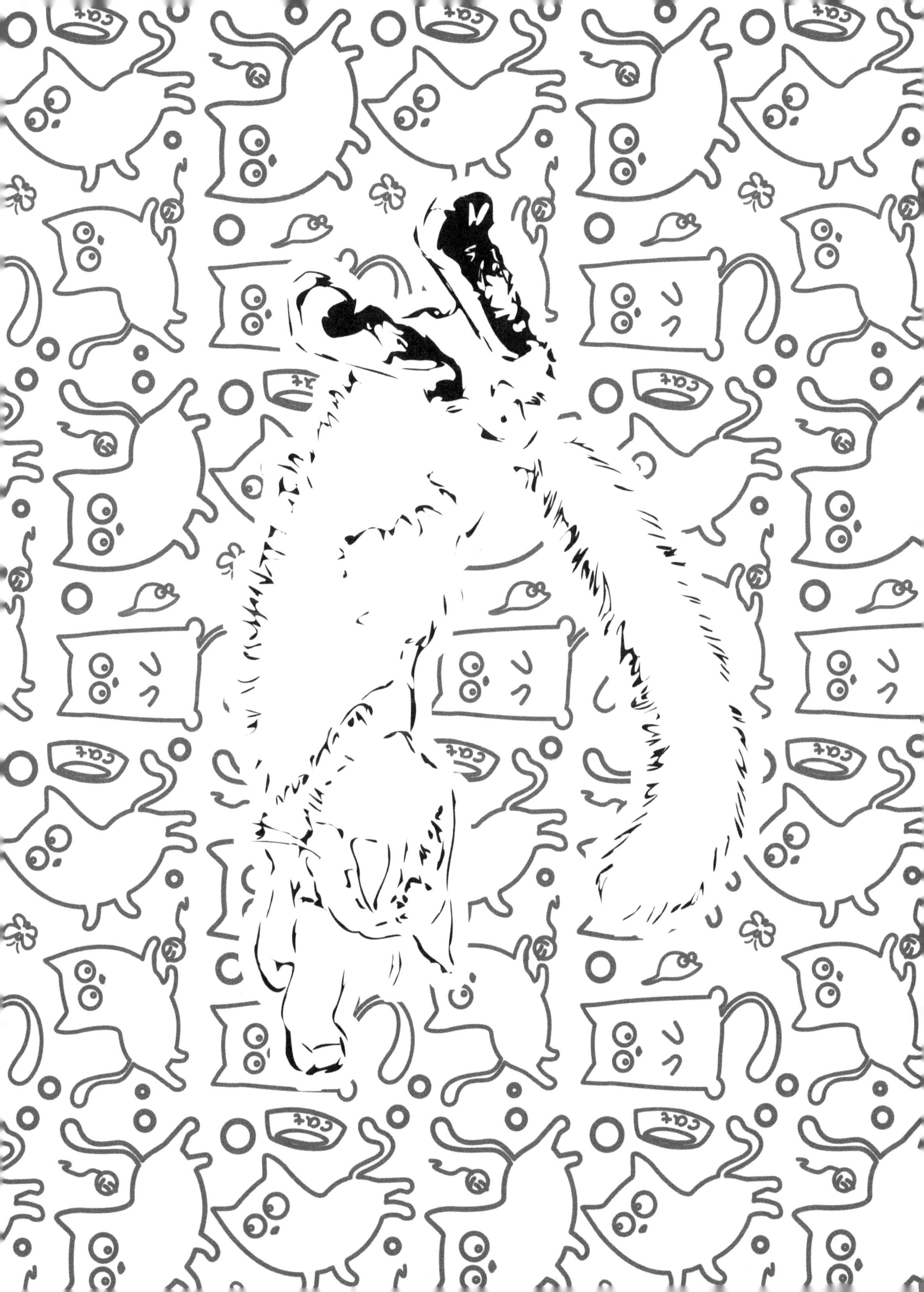

www.ingramcontent.com/pod-product-compliance
Lightning Source LLC
Chambersburg PA
CBHW081631220526
45468CB00009B/2385
* 9 7 8 1 7 2 4 2 5 4 3 7 5 *